WE STICK TOGETHER

LESSONS LEARNED FROM COMMANDING USS THE SULLIVANS (DDG-68)

TONY PARISI

ISBN 978-1-66781-116-1 eBook 978-1-66781-117-8

ACKNOWLEDGMENTS

THANK YOU TO MY FAMILY (Joy, Madison, Dylan, & João) for giving me the time and space to capture these lessons learned. I would also like to thank all the crew members past and present of USS THE SULLIVANS (DDG-68) and (DD-537); the USS THE SULLIVANS Foundation; and Miss Kelly Sullivan Loughren, the ship's sponsor. Your dedication and effort means so much to all of us who had the privilege to serve aboard these historic ships.

My sources for the stories, events, and facts herein come from my own memories, my captain's journal, and other unclassified documents I kept from my time in command. Everything in this work is the truth as I understood it to be. Any misrepresentations, misquotations, or mistakes are due to unintentional human error. Please let me know, and forgive me my trespasses.

I purposefully avoided using real names throughout this effort with the exception of those named Sullivan, senior civilian and military leaders in the public domain, and some of my own family members. The people I describe in these pages are real and had a major impact on my life and those of our crew. I acknowledge that there were many more lessons learned and too many great people I served with in USS THE SULLIVANS (DDG-68) to mention. I did not leave anyone out on purpose.

A special thanks to my grandfather Antonio Ribeiro and my father James F. Parisi who are both gone but not forgotten. Their guidance and actions continue to influence my thinking and conduct in positive ways. Thank you, Mom, Maria Parisi, for making me go to church, influencing me to attend Norwich University, and encouraging me to pursue a career in the U.S. Navy. All your hard work, selfless efforts, and love made me who I am today. Thank you.

Also thank you to my sister Jennifer, my brother Matthew, and all our family and friends from Gloucester, MA. Your love, support, and enthusiasm helped me greatly along this journey.

Thank you. *Muito Obrigado. Molte Grazie.*

Captain Tony Parisi, USN (Ret)
Ponte Vedra, Florida
August 2021

CONTENTS

PREFACE

I wanted to write this book to provide readers insight into what it means to serve aboard a historic U.S. Navy ship, USS THE SULLIVANS (DDG-68) and share some valuable lessons learned. In the U.S. Navy, after every evolution, event, mission, and deployment, someone is tasked with writing down the lessons learned. These lessons learned serve as corporate knowledge and wisdom for future generations of sailors. They are a treasure trove of history, stories, and facts and serve as the repository of sea-going culture. Lessons learned are gained through sacrifice and huge expenditures of time and money. They are important and should be read, understood, and used by those who want to succeed at sea and in life.

We Stick Together, is the title of this work and the official motto of USS THE SULLIVANS (DDG-68). This simple phrase uttered in late 1941 by five American brothers from Waterloo, Iowa is also the theme of this book. George, Francis, Joseph, Madison, and Albert Sullivan had to petition the U.S. Navy to allow them to serve together in the same ship. They did this out of love for one another and because, as they said, "We have always fought for each other; and now we want to continue to fight side by side."[1]

We Stick Together is more than a motto, phrase, or bumper sticker. These three simple words spoken from the heart so many years ago

---

1 John R. Satterfield, We Band of Brothers: The Sullivans and World War II, Mid-Prairie Books 1995, p.55.

carry much truth and wisdom for all of us today. Serving one's country at sea in peacetime, and especially during World War II required sacrifice and selflessness. The Sullivan brothers were ordinary Americans who perished at sea fighting side by side. Their tragic loss inspired our nation to fight on and win, and continues to inspire all those who serve the United States of America today.

This is the story from my time in command of USS THE SULLIVANS (DDG-68) from June 2006 to December 2007. During this 18-month snapshot of time, USS THE SULLIVANS (DDG-68) sailed the seven seas combatting terrorism, training with allies, and proudly demonstrating to the world what happens when *We Stick Together*.

I hope you will enjoy reading about our adventures and the lessons learned as much as the crew and I enjoyed living through them. Thank you for your time and readership.

CHAPTER 1

CHANGE OF COMMAND, UNDERWAY SHIFT COLORS

USS THE SULLIVANS (DDG-68) underway circa 2006

"All lines on deck, underway, shift colors, sound one prolonged blast," announced the officer of the deck as USS THE SULLIVANS (DDG-68) got underway from Naval Station Mayport, Florida bound for Her Majesty's Naval Base Clyde, Faslane, Scotland. It was June 5, 2006 and aboard the billion-dollar, Aegis guided missile destroyer named in honor of the five Sullivan brothers from Waterloo, Iowa, were 300 crew members, the off going captain, me, and our wives. The then commanding officer of the ship had decided to conduct the change of command at sea; and the only guests permitted were the off going and on coming captains' spouses. This was his prerogative and decision. Based on the ship's schedule, it was also the least disruptive and most appropriate venue for this time-honored event required by regulation and over 230 years of U.S. Naval tradition.

Reflecting on that day now, I imagine the crew had many questions running through their minds. The captain of a modern U.S. warship has great influence and impact on the day-to-day lives, aspirations, and careers of the sailors in his or her care. One evaluation, phone call, or email by the commanding officer could change the arc of a Sailor's career. What kind of person and leader would the new commanding officer be? Will he be a screamer who worries more about his own career and fitness report rather than the needs of his sailors? Would he avoid or freeze up in stressful situations? Would he be competent, fair, and selfless or cruel, nepotistic, and self-centered? On June 5, 2006, I did not worry about such questions as I was fulfilling the major career milestone every surface warfare officer (SWO) strives for: command at sea. Life seemed to be moving so fast then that I did not have time to think about long-term issues such as how command of this ship would impact my character, my family, and my future. The time for reflecting on such questions would come much later. On this unseasonally cool and breezy North Florida morning my mind was focused on the task at hand: assuming responsibility for 300 sailors and the billion-dollar warship named after five American heroes.

The change-of-command ceremony was conducted professionally in working uniforms on the ship's flight deck. Most of the ship's crew not on watch were gathered and standing in ranks, their boots holding them fast in place on the non-skid surface of the flight deck as the hull wallowed slowly in the rolling seas. The ship was steaming eastward at bare steerageway (i.e., about 3 knots) within sight of the coast of Jacksonville Beach. The bridge team adjusted course to keep the winds to a minimum across the flight deck. There were no chairs, bunting, or frill. USS THE SULLIVANS (DDG-68) was haze gray and underway. Sea water spray and diesel exhaust clung around my head. My mouth was dry and my undershirt was damp with sweat. I was both excited and nervous but trying hard not to show signs of either state to the crew. The ship's executive officer ran and emceed the ceremony, standing behind a well-used wooden podium with a single microphone and USS THE SULLIVANS logo attached to it. He flipped through a white binder with clear plastic sleeves protecting the pages, and followed the change-of-command script as required by U.S. Navy regulations.

The formalities of the simple change-of-command ceremony lasted less than 30 minutes. The event was professionally executed, short and to the point. The off-going captain said a few words of thanks to the crew and his wife and then read his orders. I read my orders and took command of THE SULLIVANS at sea, a mile or so off the coast of Mayport, Florida. I did not feel any different, but I was now the commanding officer of USS THE SULLIVANS (DDG-68) and responsible for all souls onboard and the good order and discipline of a crew I did not know yet.

Shortly after the ceremony ended, the offgoing former commanding officer, his wife, and my bride walked to the edge of the flight deck. It was time for them to go home. The appropriate flight deck safety nets were carefully lowered to open a path from the deck edge to the pitching and rolling sea tractor tug that would take them back to terra firma.

I watched as some small whitecaps lapped both the tug and USS THE SULLIVANS (DDG-68). The seas were rolling a bit more now. We were at sea in the Atlantic during hurricane season and the winds were picking up. I kissed my wife goodbye and watched as she waited for the right moment to jump to the plastic orange steps of the swinging, rope ladder on the bobbing sea tractor tug. She looked frightened, but this was the only way home. She had no other option and had to get back to our two young children. She told me later that she was scared that if she jumped and missed she could fall between the tug and our ship and be crushed and disappear beneath the waves. I knew she could make the jump easily and did not realize until much later how frightening this experience was for her at the time.

As I watched my wife make it safely aboard the tug and head back into port, I turned my attention to the immediate task at hand: commanding USS THE SULLIVANS (DDG-68). I would not see her and my two young children for two months. Long absences from loved ones were not unusual for U.S. Navy sailors. Neither was compartmentalizing emotions and feelings, tucking them deep down inside to be dealt with sometime in the future, when the ship and all its responsibilities and worries were safely tied to a pier and someone else's charge. I knew that I would miss my family, but in that moment I did not feel it. I only felt compelled to get to the bridge and ensure that we got the ship four hours ahead of PIM (plan of intended movement) in order to gain some time to conduct training as we crossed the Atlantic.

U.S. Navy ships have to file MOVREPs (movement reports) prior to sailing so that they can be tracked via the Navy World Wide Military Command and Control System. This practice was initiated as a lesson learned following the tragic loss of the USS INDIANAPOLIS (CA-35). USS

INDIANAPOLIS (CA-35) was a Portland-class heavy cruiser tasked with carrying parts of the first nuclear weapon, Little Boy, to be used in war to the island of Tinian in the Pacific. On July 30, 1945, USS INDIANAPOLIS (CA-35) was torpedoed by a Japanese submarine and sank. Her crew numbered nearly 1,200 sailors. Three hundred Indie sailors went down with the ship, but almost 900 survived the initial attack and took to the sea in life boats, life jackets, or clinging to floating debris. However, because the ship had been conducting a very sensitive mission, its movements were kept secret and not shared with the appropriate U.S. Navy officials, who did not realize the ship was over-due. After several days lost at sea, only 316 sailors survived while the majority suffered horrible deaths from exposure, dehydration, and shark attacks.

The tragedy of USS INDIANAPOLIS (CA-35) faded from the minds of most Americans for many years until it resurfaced in the character of Captain Quint, the hard hearted shark hunter and skipper of the *Orca* in the movie *Jaws,* who was a fictional survivor of USS INDIANAPOLIS (CA-35). Peter Benchley's novel about a killer shark became Steven Spieldberg's blockbuster 1975 film *Jaws*, which scared many Americans from entering the ocean. The fear and horror that the survivors of USS INDIANAPOLIS (CA-35) faced in 1945 was not from a single animatronic shark but dozens, possibly even hundreds of real White Tipped and Tiger sharks. The survivors had to fend off constant shark attacks without the benefit of Captain Quint's harpoons, scuba tanks, or rifle. Well over a hundred men were eaten alive like Captain Quint all because no one knew their ship's voyage plan.

The MOVREP system allowed U.S. Navy ships to be up to four hours ahead or four hours behind their plan of intended movement. Most U.S. Navy commanding officers like to keep their ships four hours ahead of PIM so that they have time and space to train. Had the MOVREP system been in place in 1942, it might have saved at least one of the Sullivan brothers and certainly would have saved many more of the USS INDIANAPOLIS (CA-35) crew. MOVREPs were a costly lesson learned, which benefit all U.S. Navy sailors today.

When the captain enters the bridge of a U.S. Navy warship, the first person to see him or her annouces, "Captain on the bridge." It is a very strange thing to hear this phrase and then realize that you are in fact the captain. There is no one coming to mentor or assist you anymore. It is just you and you alone. I knew the officers on watch that day wanted to make a good first impression on their new captain. The boatswain mate of the watch spotted me early and announced my arrival. I wanted to high-five him, but that would not have been appropriate so I stoically and calmly walked to the chart table and then climbed into the captain's chair. My heart rate and blood pressure were elevated, as was my satisfaction with my new job. I looked out at the horizon about seven miles away. I was calm but also a bit anxious. I wanted to enjoy this moment, but I knew there was a mountain of work to do, including releasing the official messages regarding the change of command as well as planning for the days upcoming training events. For that brief moment, however, I chose to just sit still and listen to the orders being given by the personnel on watch and stare at the grayish blue horizon in front of me. It was only 10:30 in the morning, but it felt like late afternoon.

I had achieved my career goal of becoming the commanding officer of a U.S. Navy destroyer. I felt even more fortunate for having been selected to command this particular historic warship, named after the five Sullivan brothers. It had taken so long to get here, but time also seemed to accelerate in the few final months before this day. As the ship heaved and pitched in the seas, I relaxed into my chair and retraced the long journey to command in my mind. The familiar whine of the two General Electric LM 2500 gas turbine engines on line served as pleasant white noise. USS THE SULLIVANS (DDG-68) was at split plant (one engine per shaft) and was cruising at 20 knots, heading out across the vast expanse of the Atlantic Ocean. There were no other vessels in sight and land was fading fast astern of us. I had been on the bridge of destroyers many times in the past, but never as the commanding officer. The adventure of a lifetime had just begun.

CHAPTER 2

THE JOURNEY TO COMMAND

Ensign Tony Parisi USS FORRESTAL (CV-59) New York City 1989

Captain Tony Parisi, fifth and final command 2015 Monterey, CA

My official journey to USS THE SULLIVANS (DDG-68) began one year prior to the change of command on June 5, 2006. In June 2005, I was in my third year ashore as a senior instructor at the Surface Warfare Officer School (SWOS) Command in Newport, Rhode Island. The mission of SWOS was based on the famous words of Admiral Arleigh Burke, "This ship is built to fight. You had better know how." It was my job to bring new commanding and executive officers up to speed on the latest tactics, techniques, and procedures to successfully fight and win at sea. The training culminated with a week-long ship ride at sea. My colleagues and me would serve as the students' escorts during these ship familiarization rides. I participated in over a dozen and learned something new on each one.

Being a SWOS instructor meant earning a master training specialist qualification, which would prove to be a valuable commodity after my Navy career came to a close. Most importantly, serving as a surface warfare instructor allowed my colleagues and me to focus on the latest operations and changes regarding U.S. Navy surface combatants. As a career surface warfare officer, I could think of no better place to prepare for my own future command at sea tour.

Living and working in Newport, RI, was enjoyable as well as professionally rewarding. Newport was a tourist attraction for both New Yorkers and Bostonians. It was home to many famous mansions, including the Elms, Rosecliff, Chateau-sur-Mer, and the Marble House, the former summer residence of the Vanderbilts. I grew up less than 100 miles to the north in America's oldest fishing port, Gloucester, MA, and spent time in Newport as a boy when our family fishing trawler was built and launched at the former Direktor shipyard on Narragansett Bay. Newport would be the closest we would be stationed to my family and my boyhood home for my entire 29 years of active duty service.

On June 28, 2005, I was playing Wiffle ball with my young son in our home-made Fenway Park-style miniature ball field created with a borrowed lawn mower and the use of U.S. Navy housing fence line serving as the Green Monster (i.e., the left field wall at Fenway Park in Boston, MA). My wife, Joy, called me into the house and pushed the silver button underneath the little blinking red light on our answering machine, and I heard my boss, Captain C's voice gleefully announce, "Ding, Ding, Ding, Ding, THE SULLIVANS arriving ..."[2] This was good-natured surface warfare parlance signifying that I had been selected to command USS THE SULLIVANS (DDG-68). Captain C was proud and happy for Joy and me, and took sincere pleasure in delivering this long-awaited great news. I remember standing there stunned, like how I felt when I watched the Boston Red Sox win their first World Series in more than 86 years in 2004. USS THE SULLIVANS (DDG-68) was the exact ship I wanted in the homeport we requested. I had hoped that I would be fortunate enough to be selected to command USS THE SULLIVANS (DDG-68) but had prepared our family for wherever the needs of the Navy would take us. Perhaps it was the luck of the Irish, or maybe preparation and opportunity, that had favored us this time around. Either way my family and I were thrilled and excited about heading to USS THE SULLIVANS (DDG-68) and moving to Florida.

In the days and weeks prior to receiving the good news about THE SULLIVANS I believe the universe had provided some foreshadowing of my selection. During a ship ride in San Diego, California I had

---

2 Ding, Ding, Ding, Ding signifies four bells, the formal announcement on a ship's 1MC signifying the captain (or an officer of the rank of O-5) has come aboard or departed.

befriended a sailor who had served in USS THE SULLIVANS (DDG-68). I did not mention to him that I hoped to be selected for command of THE SULLIVANS only that I was aware of the unique name and history of the ship. He spoke at length of the great camaraderie and team spirit of THE SULLIVANS that arose from the ship's motto, *We Stick Together.* At the time, I didn't think this encounter anything more than just a coincidence, but for some reason it inspired me to write the story down, and from that day forward I began keeping a journal all the way through command. A few weeks later I learned that two new enlisted sailors had reported to SWOS from USS THE SULLIVANS (DDG-68). One of them became my neighbor in Navy housing, yet another sign from the universe. After pondering these prophetic events, my wife and I discussed how earlier that summer while attending a Newport Gulls baseball game, our family had used some random seat cushions that had USS THE SULLIVANS (DDG-68) stickers on them.[3]

Could all these events be random coincidences or was the universe trying to tell us something? I had worked at sea for most of my teenage and adult life. I believed in hard work and the passionate pursuit of one's goals. I was raised to believe in the American dream; and that success in life required continual learning, helping others, and maintaining focus on one's goals. The most scientific and rational explanation I could think of was that my connecting of all the signs with a link to THE SULLIVANS, was my subconscious mind taking notice of that which I desired. Today I prefer to believe that our lives and the universe are inexplicably connected, and the signs that my wife and I noted were our prayers being answered by providence: "ask, and it shall be given to you, seek and

---

3 The Newport Gulls are a baseball club in the New England Collegiate Baseball league. They play at Cardines Field in Newport, Rhode Island, one of the oldest ballparks in the United States.

you shall find, knock and it shall be opened to you."[4] In the end, the universe and my detailer (the person that provides official orders for your next tour of duty) had given me exactly what I had asked for: a chance to command USS THE SULLIVANS (DDG-68). I would commit my entire being to this endeavor, which I had wanted for so long. I planned to remain optimistic and to accept the things to which fate binds you, and love the people with whom fate brings you together, and do so with all my heart.[5] Professionally, emotionally, and spiritually I was ready for the challenge of command. But like all prospective sea captains, I had concerns and self-doubt.

On May 20, 2006, approximately ten days before I was to report aboard USS THE SULLIVANS (DDG-68), here is what I entered in my journal:

10 days left before I report aboard. Today in the world the big news is the release of the Da Vinci Code [movie]; the war in Iraq; the price of gas/oil; confirmation of General Hayden as director of the CIA; and discussion on what to do about illegal immigration at the U.S. southern border. As for myself, self-assessment has been on my mind. The Navy has ingrained in me a very distinct, problem solving habit that tends to emphasize the negative. So here goes: I am sometimes too compulsive; too loud. I ask too many questions and tend to embellish a bit when I story tell. I also seem to forget about the people that love me most in this world–perhaps not forget but under prioritize. This maybe another SWO tendency or just human nature. SWOs [surface warfare officers] sometimes treat those that serve them the best the worst. All these things I am aware of, and with God's help I will try and overcome. I have also been thinking about what I will say to the crew and when. Over time I won't worry about that

---

4 NIV Matthew 7:7.

5 This sentence is paraphrased from the famous quote from stoic philosopher and Roman Emperor, Marcus Aurelius, from his book Meditations; www.goodreads.com.

so much – at least I hope. Joy has met the current CO's [commanding officer] wife and says she seemed nice and was sincere. How will the crew take to us? Joy and I. Deep down I want them to love us and respect us right off the bat. If they don't well that should not change my pledge to them. I honestly don't fear rejection at any professional level. I really believe I can follow the courage of my convictions, but I guess I have yet to be tested. I am sure command will give me plenty of opportunities to do that.

I imagine that all prospective commanding officers have similar thoughts, concerns, and worries as they head to command. It is a stressful journey that tests your character and your family. It is not easy and there is no perfect checklist, manual, or guide on how to prepare yourself for the ups and downs that accompany command at sea. The U.S. Navy does a fantastic job training and preparing officers for the leadership and tactical skills needed to succeed at sea, but it is each sailor's responsibility to shore up their character for the challenges that will come. Humility and patience will be required. Ego, ambition, and personal desires must be securely stored for sea. Stand by for high seas and heavy rolls, for they will come.

SWOs are trained professional mariners who must be ready to fight and win wars at sea. As in any profession, SWOs earn their way to command by proving their competency over a long period of time through the achievement of specific required career milestones. For those of us who chose to serve at sea in ships of the line, demonstrating leadership, ship handling, marine engineering, tactical prowess, and administrative skills at sea at multiple levels of responsibility are essential to the journey to command. Like the sacraments in the Christian Church, these requirements must be successfully completed, documented, and witnessed by other believers before one is even considered for the sacred honor of command at sea.

Like all professions with long histories, surface warfare has a unique set of customs, practices, and traditions. One of the Navy's fundamental operating principles focuses on formality. Formality is the rigid adherence to customs, practices, and traditions. It provides structure and purpose, and demands alert watch standing; formal repeat back of verbal commands; procedural compliance; and a litany of other protocols. Over the past 230 years, the SWO community has developed a distinct professional culture, complete with its own language and peculiar customs. What follows in the next few paragraphs is my own personal observations of what it was like to be a SWO and contribute to this unique military culture from 1988 to 2017. My views of the SWO community and culture are not meant to represent all surface warfare officers. I served on many ships on the East, West, and Gulf Coasts. I never served as ship's company in ships stationed in Hawaii or overseas. Admittedly my views on SWO culture are incomplete and include some generalizations, but they do provide the reader a look behind the blue Herculite curtain separating SWOs from other U.S. Navy warfare communities such as aviation, submariners, and special warfare (aka SEALs).[6]

Surface warfare officers are determined to seek perfection in all they do. Ideally, they should be stoic sea-going warriors who operate according to the Golden Rule (i.e., do unto others as you would have them do unto you) but also the Roman saying of no better friend and no worse enemy. They will work extremely long hours just because. They are driven by a Darwinian sense of competition and also by Jewish-Catholic guilt and

---

6 The U.S. Navy special warfare community is best known for its SEAL (Sea, Air, Land) special warfare operators.

the Protestant work ethic. SWOs believe in karmic justice and the chain of command. SWOs emphasize the negative and never want to show their blemishes for fear of criticism. We can be a cantankerous and irritable lot due to long hours of watch, too much coffee, and lack of sleep. Some of us suffer from resting-bitch face as urbane and polite speech is often lost at sea. And unbeknownst to us, our non-verbal communication techniques often come across as menacing and intimidating, as I have been told on more than one occasion.

We often forget that we are the guardians of the world's seas and global trade as we tend to focus on the small details inside larger problems. As SWOs get more and more senior, they believe they can do more with less, as they have been told this all their careers. Leadership and accountability are driven into the SWO mind at a very early age. SWOs will be held accountable for their mistakes and should hold their subordinates accountable, especially when it is most difficult and uncomfortable to do so.

SWOs are expected to lead and lead at every level: division officer through flag rank. Leadership for the surface warfare officer means taking charge, organizing chaos, and executing missions. SWOs are expected to be role models for their sailors. Honor, courage, and commitment are minimum requirements for SWO junior officers. In addition, they are expected to be intelligent, professional mariners with integrity and a can-do attitude. SWOs do not tolerate hypocrisy, laziness, or lying. SWOs are supposed to be warfighters but often become generalists and grand administrators during peace-time. While there are dozens of sub-specialties in the SWO community, driving ships and leading sailors at sea are considered essential skills. Major mistakes will not be tolerated, and officers that allide,[7] collide, or run a ship aground will be let go.

Surface Warfare Officer pin - Unrestricted Line Officer 1110

SWOs are proud and often look back nostalgically at their tours, forgetting the bad times and remembering the good. When we are at sea, we often complain about the hard work and endless inspections, but once ashore we long for sea duty again. SWOs are superstitious traditionalists and crave the tribal storytelling ways of their seagoing forefathers. SWOs pride themselves on the time they have spent at sea in some of the worst parts of the globe. We sometimes speak of our near misses and wipe our brows and whisper, "there for the Grace of God go I ..." SWOs are intolerant of inactivity and a lack of initiative but grateful for subordinates who take on big tasks even if they make errors. We would rather have someone who gives 110% instead of someone with many talents who gives less. We tend to over task those among us that work the hardest, driving our most talented junior officers into other communities or civilian professions.

In the past, many SWOs seemed frustrated by a self-imposed inferiority complex. Some SWOs believed that their community was second-rate,

---

7 To allide means to hit a non-moving object at sea such as a buoy or a docked ship.

and that naval aviation, special warfare (SEALs), and submariners were higher in the food chain. Perhaps this was in part because the surface warfare community had been for a time the repository for fallen angels (i.e., naval aviators who failed out of flight school) and nuke waste (sailors who were dropped from the nuclear power training pipeline). Hollywood seemed to celebrate naval aviation with movies such as *Top Gun* and *Flight of the Intruder*. There were dozens of books and films about Navy SEALs and submariners but not much that celebrated the surface warfare community. Even the naval criminal investigative service (NCIS) and judge advocate general's corps (JAG) got TV shows while surface warfare officers toiled at sea for decades with little to no fanfare from the media.[8]

Personally, I always believed that the surface warfare community was the heart and soul of the U.S. Navy. In 1986 I was a junior at Norwich University, the Military College of Vermont. I distinctly remember my fellow students discussing which Navy community we wanted to join upon commissioning. Most Norwich students enrolled in the U.S. Navy Reserve Officer Training Corps (NROTC) program in 1986 wanted to fly F-14 Tomcats like Tom Cruise in *Top Gun*. Another group wanted to become Marines. I was clearly in the minority and only wanted to serve on ships at sea. Then as now, I could not fathom why anyone would volunteer to join the U.S. Navy and not want the same.

I realize that in the 1980s, I was blinded by what today would be considered acute surface warfare implicit bias. Admittedly I had an unconscious prejudice and predilection to the surface warfare community because of my upbringing and environment. My family life and work experience

---

8 The 1987 hit film No Way Out, starring Kevin Costner had a protagonist that was a surface warfare officer. However, Costner's character, LT Tom Farrell, turned out to be a Soviet spy.

had all revolved around going to sea. It was what I knew and loved. I had always planned on making my living at sea like my father and his father and their forefathers before them. Surface warfare provided the right path for my passion and purpose in life.

Me, my grandfather, mother, father, and brother circa 1983

F/V Gloucesterman at sea Atlantic Ocean circa 1985

My seagoing career began around 1980, when I became a crew member aboard the stern trawler *Gloucesterman*, our family's fishing vessel homeported in Gloucester. My dad, James Parisi, was the captain and part owner of a 78-foot, steel-hulled stern trawler built at Direktor Shipyards in Newport in 1979. I joined the crew and was paid half a share. Fishermen operate under a strict profit sharing system, and are paid based on what they bring in to port to sell. The catch is auctioned off upon arrival in port, and the crew get a share of the profits. I always thought this a just and fair system, and wondered why other businesses never embraced this model. The owners took the risk and got more shares, but crewmen were paid for their work and received a share of the profits of every trip. As I was just a teenager and the captain's son, I was entitled to half a share, which was fine by me.

Commercial fishing is very difficult work, with its own distinct customs, practices, and traditions. Deck hands on trawlers worked hard in arduous conditions and got very little sleep. Fishermen only earned paychecks by going to sea and successfully catching, culling, and offloading fish. There were six of us in the crew and everyone had nicknames based on their exploits, character, or habits. There was Manny Take a Pill, Wojahowitz (pronounced WO-JA-HOE-ITS from the TV show *Barney Miller*), Tommy Half a Buck, Jackie Waffle, Joe Ringo, and me. Later, when I was in college and a U.S. Navy midshipman, the crew would call me Ensign Parker, after the Tim Conway character in the TV show *McHale's Navy*. I didn't like this nickname but let them have their fun. Good-natured humor kept hubris in check and relieved the stress associated with commercial fishing, one of the most dangerous professions in the world.

Trawling in the North Atlantic meant days of around-the-clock work continuously setting out and then retrieving heavy steel ground tackle that supported a large funnel-shaped mesh net. The net would be towed at speeds of 1 to 3 knots at relatively shallow depths, 50 to 100 fathoms (one fathom equals 6 feet) along the sea floor on the continental shelf and specific underwater mesa-like banks which served as fertile fishing grounds along the eastern seaboard from northern Maine to the coasts of Long Island. The net would be dragged along the sea floor for three to five hours at a time, hopefully with its top buoyed open and its bottom chain or rollers stirring up mud and trapping fish, mollusks, and all sorts of sea creatures residing on the ocean floor. The net would then be hauled back and the contents dumped on deck to be sorted and culled. The net would then be repaired if necessary and set back out.

This process repeated itself over and over until the ice, fuel, or food gave out or enough fish were caught to make a trip.

In addition to this back-breaking cycle, commercial fishing also required routine boat maintenance, splicing line, busting rust (i.e., metal preservation), painting, engineering duties, and standing watch, and was very similar to serving at sea in the U.S. Navy. I earned the equivalent of the Officer of the Deck and Engineering Officer of the Watch qualifications by the age of 16. I stood watch, learned the rules of the road, and worked on deck and in the engine room. I loved fishing with my father and working at sea. My dad realized this, and while he would have loved for me to keep fishing with him, he could see that the best days of the fishing business were coming to an end. He wanted something better for me eventhough fishing had well provided for our family for three generations. He encouraged me to pursue an alternative career, anything I wanted but not fishing. I think I chose wisely. I became a SWO and served 29 years at sea and ashore.

My family lived in Gloucester but originated from Europe. My mother's family emigrated from Figueira da Foz, Portugal, in 1944 and my dad's from Terrasini, Sicily, in the early 1920s. Portugal and Italy at the time were both under the control of Fascist dictators—Benito Mussolini in Italy and António de Oliveira Salazar in Portugal. America offered both my grandfathers exponentially more opportunity than living under Fascism. There were probably many other reasons why they chose to make America their home (i.e., better pay, family members who previously emigrated, lower taxes, etc.), but the freedom to give their families a better shot in life was the main driver. This was not lost on me, and would influence my decision to give back and serve the country that offered hope and happiness to my family.

My grandfather on my mother's side was named Antonio Ribeiro. I was named after him and revered him ever since I can remember. He had been a fisherman all his life and had fished from wooden dories pulling long lines on the Grand Banks in the middle of the Atlantic Ocean. I remember sitting with him in our small kitchen and listening to his stories as he puffed on his Winston cigarettes and drank strong black coffee. He was a quiet, hard-working man with a selfless heart who loved his family more than himself. He never asked for much and seemed pleased and satisfied by my presence alone.

My Sicilian grandfather, Captain Matthew Parisi, was born in Gloucester upon his family's arrival from Sicily. He came from a large fishing family and also became a fisherman and later captain and owner of several fishing vessels. He was hard-working, intelligent, and, at times, intimidating. He too loved his family but did not express it with hugs or words. I admired him but never got to know him as well as I would have liked.

Fishing was all my family knew on both sides. Going to sea was what all the men I knew and respected did. It was our family's profession and purpose in life and I was proud of this sea-going heritage. I could not wait to go to sea for the first time. It all seemed quite normal to me and was all I knew.

My Portuguese and Sicillian grandfathers passed away in 1991 and 1994. My father died in 2014. I think about them often, and all that they taught me about life and working at sea. While I can't speak to them directly, their wisdom and wit come to me in my thoughts and dreams. Their spirit lives on in my heart and my memories. When I look out at the Atlantic now I can not help but smile and remember all the hard-earned lessons learned from serving with them at sea and ashore. It was grueling and exhaustive work, but it readied me for a career in the U.S. Navy and guided me on my journey to command USS THE SULLIVANS (DDG-68).

My grandparents, father, and mother all had distinctly different personalities, with their own unique peculiarities and passions, but somehow we formed a very strong family bond, like the braided wire rope used to tow fishing gear or lace up flight deck safety nets on U.S. Navy ships. Our family argued and fought like all families do from time to time, but we did stick together when it mattered most. *We Stick Together*, the motto of USS THE SULLIVANS (DDG-68) and the Sullivan brothers, reflected this exact feeling and spirit. It resonated in my mind and in my heart, and I know many in our crew felt the same despite our 300 unique biographies. This ship with its historic name and story drew us all together in a way I had never experienced before. We became a family—THE SULLIVANS family—and it felt like home.

A few years before my father passed away, he began to write poetry. He did not have a college education but he was a very perceptive, witty, and intelligent man. His simple poems would appear in our local newspaper, the *Gloucester Daily Times*, and one even earned him top prize in a local poetry contest. He realized that through poetry his legacy, thoughts, and wisdom would survive his passing. He chose poetry as the medium to convey what he considered his most important lessons learned across space and time. Here is one of his poems that conveys this love and spirit. It also reminds me that all who go to sea together become a family:

"Two Captains" a Poem by Captain James Parisi, *F/V Gloucesterman*

The Fishing Captain goes to sea

So his family won't be hungry.

The Navy Captain goes to sea

For his family and his country.

The Navy Captain has sworn an obligation.

The Fishing Captain has made fishing his occupation.

The Fishing Captain goes to sea

To seek fish in every direction.

The other goes to sea

To seek and destroy for our protection.

Now you may ask yourself—

What can these two captains possibly have in common?

One carries a net – one carries a gun.

I will answer that question for you.

You see – These two Captains are father and son.

Captains James and Anthony Parisi

The journey to command of USS THE SULLIVANS (DDG-68) was long and difficult. I am not sure I could have done it without the love and support of my family. The lesson learned here is behind every successful sailor at sea there are many enthusiastic cheerleaders and selfless supporters that enable their journeys. Many times in the rush to achieve our goals we forget how we got there and the people who helped us. *We Stick Together* reminded us all to be grateful for our friends and families and tell them thank you from time to time. We all need to cultivate the habit of gratitude. This is a very old lesson learned which first came to us more than 2,000 years ago when Marcus Tullius Cicero, the Roman statesman, scholar, and philosopher observed, "A thankful heart is not only the greatest virtue, but the parent of all other virtues."[9]

---

9 https://www.goodnet.org/articles/690 Cicero quote downloaded October 6, 2021.

It takes on average between 15 and 20 years of service for men and women to reach O-5, commander command of a U.S. Navy warship. The path begins with commissioning as an Ensign (O-1) and one long or two shorter division officer tours, which can last 36 to 48 months. Next comes the department head level, which requires at least two tours (or one longer tour) totaling a minimum of 36 months of at sea time. Following that an officer will serve as an executive officer at sea. U.S. Navy surface warfare officers must earn their Officer of the Deck (OOD), surface warfare officer (SWO) pin, Engineering Officer of the Watch (EOOW), Tactical Action Officer (TAO), and Command at Sea qualifications along the way. The Navy also requires certain shore tours for professional development, graduate education, and skill specialization. In my case this process took 18 years with three tours ashore: graduate student 1992-1994 at the Naval Postgraduate School in Monterey, CA; NATO intelligence analyst at Allied Forces South, Naples, Italy, 1999-2000; and instructor, Surface Warfare Officers School Command, Newport, RI, 2002-2005. Eighteen years of service for 18 months in command, that is the price one must pay for the opportunity to command a U.S. Navy destroyer at sea.

USS ZEPHYR (PC-8) descriptive art work

USS ZEPHYR (PC-8) decommissioning February 17, 2021 Mayport, FL

As a 30-year old lieutenant in 1997, I had the good fortune to command at sea in USS ZEPHYR (PC-8). USS ZEPHYR (PC-8) was a 178-foot, coastal patrol ship that was operated by Naval Special Warfare Command (aka SEALS). The mission of the ship was to insert and extract SEAL units into the littoral (i.e., coastal) areas of potential adversaries. This tour was so fulfilling and exciting that I committed all my professional effort and sacrificed the geographic stability of my family to pursue commander command. I was hooked and wanted to command again.

It had been almost a decade since I was in command, but the confidence and skills I learned from serving in ZEPHYR were still there. USS ZEPHYR (PC-8) was a 350-ton ship with a crew complement of 28. USS THE SULLIVANS (DDG-68) was almost 9,000 tons and well over 500 feet long (505 feet to be exact) with a crew of over 300 sailors and officers. Commander command of a multi-mission, billion-dollar plus warship is a massive responsibility. As command of USS THE SULLIVANS (DDG-68) approached, I realized just how naïve I had been during my earlier command tour. I was older now, more mature, and realized the gravity and importance of what I was committing myself and my family to. I also understood the impact that my actions and personal example would have on the men and women who made THE SULLIVANS come to life.

Commanding a U.S. Navy ship is something very few people ever get the privilege of doing. On June 5, 2006, I realized how lucky I was to have this opportunity. Only in America could a Sicilian-Portuguese son of a fisherman earn command of a billion-dollar warship named in honor of five Irish brothers who died fighting for the American dream. Taking command of USS THE SULLIVANS (DDG-68) as she steamed to Scotland felt like a lucid dream, where you become aware that you are in a dream but your thoughts and actions have some influence on the outcome.

I probably should have been nervous and scared on this first voyage with a crew I didn't know, but to my surprise I was not. The crew was well trained and highly motivated. Their camaraderie and morale were high. I felt at home and ready for the challenge. I knew this was a once-in-a-lifetime chance, and that my actions and decisions would influence the lives of my family and the crew of USS THE SULLIVANS (DDG-68) for better or for worse.

I know that my upbringing, education, and own decisions guided me on the journey to command at sea. What I could not figure out was how and why fortune, providence, or destiny led me to command this specific ship, USS THE SULLIVANS (DDG-68). I had requested command of an Arleigh Burke-class destroyer in Mayport, and hoped that it would be USS THE SULLIVANS (DDG-68), but luck and timing had never worked in my favor before when it came to orders, duty stations, or assignments. Surface warfare officers serve at the pleasure of the President of the United States and are assigned by the needs of the Navy. In 2006, the U.S. Navy had at least 47 different Arleigh Burke-class destroyers in commissioned service with several others being built in shipyards in Bath, Maine and Pascagoula, Mississippi.

I believed that USS THE SULLIVANS (DDG-68), like its predecessor USS THE SULLIVANS (DD-537), was a special and historic ship. I was drawn to it because of its name, legacy, and especially its motto. *We Stick Together* resonated in me. This simple phrase uttered by average Americans was much more profound than it appeared. *We Stick Together* is universal and true—Siamo Sempre Insieme—Juntos Somos Mais Fortes—and conveyed the same strong sentiment in English, Italian, and Portuguese. *We Stick Together* was a plan of action for five brothers but also expressed what all families, communities, and the United States needed to do when things got difficult. I wanted to know more about George, Francis, Joseph, Madison, and Albert Sullivan. Where did they come from? What were they like? What did they cherish and believe? How did they become American heroes?

CHAPTER 3

WHO WERE THE SULLIVAN BROTHERS?

The Sullivan brothers onboard USS JUNEAU (CL-52) circa 1942

The five Sullivan brothers were World War II Sailors of Irish-American descent who joined the U.S. Navy together after the attack on Pearl Harbor December 7, 1941. George, Francis, Joseph, Madison, and Albert were from America's heartland, Waterloo, Iowa. They were all killed when their ship, USS JUNEAU (CL-52) was torpedoed by a Japanese submarine at the Naval Battle of Guadalcanal on November 13, 1942. The deaths of these young brothers, ages 20-27, shocked and saddened the nation, but also motivated millions of Americans to buy war bonds, fight on, and win World War II.

By all accounts, the Sullivan brothers were typical American young men of their era. They rode motorcycles, worked low-paying jobs, drank beer, and sought the company of young ladies. They were no better or no worse than most Americans of their day. Their ordinary lives took an extraordinary turn following the Japanese attack on Pearl Harbor, Hawaii, when they learned a friend of theirs from Iowa, named Bill Ball, had been killed aboard USS ARIZONA (BB-39). Like many of their fellow Americans, the Sullivans decided to join the military and serve their country in time of need. George and Francis (aka Frank) Sullivan enlisted in the U.S. Navy in 1937. Their tour of duty was over by the time of the Pearl Harbor attack, but they clearly influenced Joseph, Madison, and Albert on joining the Navy. Their only stipulation on enlisting in the U.S. Navy was that they be allowed to serve together at sea. This was not an unusual request at the time, and there were many sets of brothers who served together in all branches of the U.S. military from its inception up to World War II.

Dr. John Satterfield's book *We Band of Brothers: The Sullivans and World War II* and the 1944 film *The Fighting Sullivans*, directed by Lloyd Bacon, are great references that provide many details of the Sullivan brothers' upbringing and story. There are thousands of other books, articles, and documents that mention the Sullivan brothers readily available online. A quick Google search lists over 47,100,000 entries for the Sullivan brothers.[10]

---

10 Google search using "The Sullivan Brothers" conducted May 25, 2021, yielded 47,100,000 results.

I tried to read, watch, and digest as much as I could about the Sullivan brothers. I wanted to know them so our crew could honor their legacy through our actions, words, and deeds. Sailors will work harder and do more for those they like and care about. George, Francis, Joseph, Madison, and Albert were transformed into heroic figures by their tragic end and a war time U.S. Government that needed heroes. Some armchair historians have taken the cynical view that the memory of the Sullivans was exploited to be used as propaganda and sell war bonds. And that is certainly one way to look at how their story was spun after they were lost. But there was another side to this story. It was personal and real and needed to be better understood by all of us in USS THE SULLIVANS (DDG-68).

We were all U.S. Navy sailors serving in a ship named in their honor. The Sullivans demonstrated patriotism, courage, and brotherly love when they chose to serve their country when they believed it was most needed. They volunteered together and were not drafted. They wanted to serve on a warship likely to see combat, which theirs did. They were hard workers and fighters. Had the Sullivans been born in Gloucester they would have fit right in. They probably would have fished together like my family did. The stories I read and the hardship they faced in their youth sounded very similar to the stories I had heard from my grandfathers and father. The Sullivans were no worse and no better than any of us. They chose to become U.S. Navy sailors after the attack on Pearl Harbor, just as many in our crew had done following the 9/11 attacks on the World Trade Center and the Pentagon 60 years later. This was my perception of the Sullivan brothers, and as my tour in their ship progressed so did my understanding of their true heroism.

While conducting my research on George, Francis, Joseph, Madison, and Albert Sullivan I learned some interesting truths. For example, contrary to popular belief the 1998 block buster movie *Saving Private Ryan* starring Tom Hanks and Matt Damon is not based on the Sullivan brothers but another group of Irish-American brothers named Niland from Tonawanda, New York.

Edward	Preston	Robert	Fredrick
(1912-1984)	(1915-1944)	(1919-1944)	(1920-1983)

The Niland Brothers from Tonawanda, NY served
in the U.S. Army during World War II

The Niland brothers—Edward, Preston, Robert, and Frederick— also served in World War II. Three of the brothers—Robert, Preston, and Edward—were believed to have been killed in action, which caused their remaining brother, Fredrick (aka Fritz) to be shipped back to the U.S. so that the Niland family wouldn't lose all of their sons following the tragedy of the Sullivan family. Edward, who was originally thought dead, was later found alive after escaping a Japanese prison camp in Burma, leaving two surviving brothers out of the four who fought in the war.[11]

In his 1998 masterpiece, *Saving Private Ryan*, Director Steven Spielberg based Matt Damon's character, James Francis Ryan, on Fritz Niland, and set the plot in June 1944 following the D-day landings vice the sea battle off Guadalcanal in November 1942. In the film, James Francis Ryan was from Paton, Iowa, vice New York (the Nilands were from New York state). Paton, Iowa, is about 120 miles west of Waterloo, Iowa. Both Private Ryan's hometown and his middle name seem to be purposefully tied to the better known story of the Sullivan brothers. It seems clear that director Steven Spielberg was aware of the Sullivans' story, as it is specifically mentioned in the film during a brief scene that takes place at the War Department in Washington as secretaries are busily typing and reading letters about to be sent to the families of the deceased. The Sullivan brothers are mentioned by name as the reason why they had to save Private Ryan, to prevent another similar thing from happening to the fictional Ryan family.

The Sullivans' story clearly added dramatic effect and purpose to *Saving Private Ryan* even though it was a minor reference. Steven Spielberg mixed elements of the Sullivan story with the Niland brothers' story to enhance the plot, linking his protagonist to the American heartland and the traditional values of the American Midwest. *Saving Private Ryan* earned five Oscars and over 500 million dollars in revenue for Spielberg and the film production companies involved. Its realistic battle scenes depicting the fear and horror of actual combat moved veterans and civilian movie-goers alike. I have seen the film several times and learn

---

11 https://www.mentalfloss.com/
article/65611/15-fascinating-facts-about-saving-private-ryan

something new with each viewing. But in the end, it is a highly polished, fictionalized representation of history. The characters in the film are not real and the emotions they convey are not sincere. Steven Spielberg, Tom Hanks, Matt Damon, Tom Sizemore, Vin Diesel, Giovanni Ribisi, and all the other fine actors made *Saving Private Ryan* feel very real but it was not.

USS JUNEAU (CL-52) Atlanta Class Light Cruiser circa 1942

USS THE SULLIVANS (DD-537) circa 1962

USS THE SULLIVANS (DDG-68) circa 2006

Saving Private Ryan is a great action movie loosely based on historical events, but the Sullivans' story is real, and the true pain of their loss was felt by their family, the community of Waterloo and the entire nation. According to Dr. Satterfield's research, the Sullivan brothers allegedly told their Navy recruiter, "We have always fought for each other; and now we want to continue to fight side by side."[12] *We Stick Together* became the motto of two ships named in honor of the Sullivan brothers: DD-537 and DDG-68. Their true story, fighting spirit, and brotherly love inspired thousands of U.S. Navy sailors who had the good fortune to serve aboard ships named in their honor.

The Sullivan brothers' story makes USS THE SULLIVANS, both DD-537, currently a floating museum in Buffalo, New York, and DDG-68, the Aegis-guided missile destroyer currently homeported in Mayport both standout from the rest of the fleet. These ships are special. Both ships

12 John R. Satterfield, We Band of Brothers: The Sullivans and World War II, Mid-Prairie Books, Parkersburg, Iowa, 1995, p.55.

have unique, detailed histories and connections with the Sullivan family from Waterloo. In addition, there are several attributes that other U.S. Navy ships simply do not have. For example, there is the official name of the ship: THE SULLIVANS. DD-537 and DDG-68 are the only U.S. Navy ships that use the definite article as part of their official name. Many sailors and civilians get this wrong. They will refer to the ship as simply SULLIVANS, and every crewmember from E-1 to O-5 instantly points their error out. It is "THE" SULLIVANS; don't forget the "THE."

There have been many U.S. Navy ships named for families and several members of the same family. I served in USS JOHN RODGERS (DD-983), which was named for Commodore John Rogers, his son, and later a grandson of the same family. USS ROOSEVELT (DDG-80) is named in honor of former presidents Theodore Roosevelt and Franklin D. Roosevelt, who were distant cousins, as well as former First Lady Eleanor Roosevelt.

The "THE" in THE SULLIVANS official name and crest honors the collective memories and contributions of five brothers' whose motto was, *We Stick Together*. The use of the definite article in this one ship's name makes it different, and reflects the U.S. Navy's tradition of independent thinking and action. Both USS THE SULLIVANS, DD-537 and DDG-68, were officially authorized to have a large green shamrock displayed prominently on both sides of their stacks. Even the Irish Navy does not allow this. There are many U.S. Navy ships with Irish names and heraldry, but only one today that is authorized to display a shamrock as part of its official paint scheme.

USS THE SULLIVANS (DDG-68) in drydock

USS THE SULLIVANS (DD-537) pierside Buffalo, NY

THE SULLIVANS is also the only ship in the fleet that consistently painted its name in green on the stern sheet. While some ships have done similar things from time to time, USS THE SULLIVANS (DDG-68) has maintained this tradition up to the present. The green paint scheme was done in homage to the Sullivans' Irish ancestry by one of the ship's first commanding officers and continued over time by those who followed, including me. I am not sure if this splash of color is officially authorized in writing, but it has long been tacitly endorsed by U.S. Navy senior leaders as a positive display of fighting spirit and camaraderie. And while this simple dash of color may appear cosmetic and trivial to outsiders, for the crew it is not. It is one of the small details that sets THE SULLIVANS apart from the rest of the fleet. It is a symbol, which like the ship's motto, *We Stick Together*, reflects a much deeper and noble purpose to those of us who have served in DD-537 or DDG-68. The Sullivan brothers' spirit lives on through the green paint, definite article, and the simple motto. All these things remind us that we are no different than they were. We are all sailors and part of a seagoing family, just like the Sullivan brothers.

We Stick Together is the perfect theme for U.S. Navy sailors. It represents the spirit of America: united we stand, divided we fall. It conveys that we are all in this together and that when we are at sea all we have is each other. Serving on a U.S. Navy destroyer at sea is difficult, hard work. Camaraderie and teamwork are required to survive and thrive in this environment. The Sullivan brothers' supreme sacrifice embodies this commitment and calls out *We Stick Together* from the hereafter. It is a call to action and became USS THE SULLIVANS (DDG-68) motto and war cry. It reminds us all that at sea we are a fraternity and family, that we are committed to stick together through high seas, bad weather, and war if required. We do this not for fame or glory but for one another as George, Francis, Joseph, Madison, Albert, and their motto proclaim.

CHAPTER 4

WHY MOTTOS MATTER

USS LAWRENCE (DDG-4) official motto "DON'T GIVE UP THE SHIP"

The word "motto" comes to us from the Latin noun, "muttum," which means a mutter or a grunt. Later the word evolved into Italian as "motto" with the meaning changing to a witty saying or watchword. Today dictionary.com defines a motto as, "a maxim adopted as an expression of the guiding principle of a person or organization, city, etc." [13]

Mottos are much more than just mutters, grunts, or witty sayings; they carry meaning and reflect the most influential and dominant values of an

---

13 https://www.dictionary.com/browse/motto

individual, team, organization, or nation. For example, the United States' official motto is *E Pluribus Unum*, which translates to "out of many, one." This simple Latin phrase exemplifies who we were at our founding, who we are today, and how we should act going forward.

Mottos matter because they simplify and encapsulate values and goals. They also transcend time and space. A good motto is simple and easy to remember and should link an individual to his or her deepest values. It provides a binding roadmap for where a team, ship, or people are going in the future. Mottos provide good self-talk for organizations and individuals and purposeful mantras that remind us of our mission and purpose. Mottos can also be used to change habits, inspire, increase productivity, motivate, and focus the mind.

Many memorable mottos come to us in Latin and foreign languages. A couple of foreign mottos that should sound familiar are the French Revolution's "Liberté, égalité, fraternité" (liberty, equality, fraternity) and Brazil's national motto "Ordem e Progresso" (Order and Progress). Because mottos convey values and illuminate a way forward, they are not bound by any particular language. As Americans, we are all familiar with the mottos "Don't Give Up the Ship," "Duty, Honor, Country," "Live Free or Die," and "Don't Tread on Me." These mottos convey the same deep meaning in any language. Mottos are charged with emotion, history, and passion. When they are uttered by leaders who believe what they are saying, they can be used as powerful tools for action: good or evil.

Gates of Auschwitz concentration camp in Poland

One infamous motto, which was used for evil purposes and that many have heard or seen but might not want to remember is "Arbeit Macht Frei." This motto means "work makes you free" in German, and it appeared over the gates of Nazi World War II concentration camps, most notably Auschwitz and Dachau. The Nazis (short for National Socialists) used this well-known motto to dupe innocent people into working hard through false hope to further their evil purposes. Here too mottos were harnessed to motivate people but not for good.

Mottos are effective because they can be remembered and built upon in peoples' minds. All people everywhere think in words. Before there can be action there has to be thought. Our thoughts begin as words. Our words ultimately become our deeds. Our deeds become our habits, and our habits, collectively, become our culture. Control the way people think and you can control their actions. Or more subtly, influence the way people think, and you can influence their actions. Memorable phrases, slogans, and mottos influence us all whether we know it or not. It is our responsibility to maintain a questioning attitude about everything, even mottos.

Words, slogans, and mottos matter. The words we hear and think about will influence each one of us. A steady stream of half-truths and little white lies can lead to destruction and even genocide. British author Eric Blair (aka George Orwell) foretold of mass manipulation by authoritarian leaders through the bending of language and the creation of new words. I learned about George Orwell in middle school and read *Animal Farm, 1984,* and other similar dystopian novels in high school and college. I learned that words, and especially mottos, were charged with emotion and could sway people into action for good or for ill.

Throughout my naval career, I knew that every email, message, memo, standing order, evaluation, or fitness report I wrote would greatly influence sailors. I tried my best to convey what I believed to be the truth at the time, but I know I did not always get it right. I too have been motivated by mottos throughout my service at sea. I still remember many of the mottos of my ships, several of which are stitched into ballcaps, polo shirts, and plaques that I keep as treasured souvenirs of my service. We all must examine if the mottos we follow are truthful and good. What mottos should I believe and follow? It is up to each of us to figure that out.

The U.S. Navy has understood the importance of mottos since its very beginning. "Don't Give Up the Ship" has been used as a motto for many U.S. Navy vessels, including USS LAWRENCE (DDG-4), the ship named in honor of Captain James Lawrence, who in 1813 muttered the phrase as his last words during the fight to save his ship, USS CHESAPEAKE.

All U.S. Navy ships are named and given mottos by the secretary of the Navy. Names and mottos personify and infuse life into inanimate steel hulls. The office of the secretary of the Navy goes to great lengths to find the right ship sponsors and christen a ship as if it were a new-born child. It does this out of tradition and with a purpose. It could be argued that naming and christening ships is the most important task of this high office. Many notable former secretaries of the Navy, such as Josephus Daniels, Charles F. Adams, William Franklin Knox, and James Forrestal, have been honored by having their names bestowed on ships of the line or whole classes of new ships. This demonstrates just how much mottos truly matter to our leaders and our Navy.

As a U.S. Navy sailor for over 29 years, I served on many ships with memorable mottos. My first ship was USS FORRESTAL (CV-59). Its motto was "First in Defense," as it was the first U.S. Navy supercarrier, designed to handle modern jet aircraft. My next ship was USS JACK WILLIAMS (FFG-24). Its motto was "Guardez Bien," which is French for "Guard Well." As a commanding officer, I was fortunate to lead two ships with fantastic mottos, which motivated the entire crew and summarized our command philosophy in three simple words. My first command at sea was USS ZEPHYR (PC-8); and its motto was "Leading the Charge." Our crew understood this to mean that we should set the example for others to follow; and be prepared to enter the fray first. USS ZEPHYR (PC-8), along with USS SQUALL (PC-7), were the first and only U.S. Navy Patrol Coastal (PC) class ships to circumnavigate the continent of South America. USS ZEPHYR (PC-8) earned back-to-back battle efficiency awards and multiple CNO (Chief of Naval Operations) safety awards, setting the example for others to follow. I can attest that our simple motto helped inspire us to achieve these feats.

My next command was USS THE SULLIVANS (DDG-68). THE SULLIVANS has what I now consider the best motto I had ever heard for sailors, which is *"We Stick Together."* I must admit when I first heard this motto I thought it was good but also simple, trite, and possibly fabricated. As I began to investigate the facts surrounding the life and tragedy of the Sullivan brothers I realized the true wisdom of this simple motto. *We Stick Together* is a self-explanatory motto for Sailors on liberty in a foreign port or in peril on the sea. It also conveys for those of us who wore this motto on our ballcaps, belt buckles, and t-shirts something much deeper. USS THE SULLIVANS (DD-537) and (DDG-68) sailors were part of a special fraternity, a sea going family that put mission first and who remained selfless and true to our nation, our navy, and one another. In time *We Stick Together* would take on much more meaning for me personally. These three simple words would connect our crew with our ship's legacy and commitment to excellence. Today when I hear someone say, *"We Stick Together"* vivid images, thoughts, and feelings flood and ebb in my soul. These three simple words would motivate me to command at sea and ashore. They would inspire me to focus on my family, my future, and to write this book.

Don't Give Up the Ship and *We Stick Together* were simple words uttered by real people that reflected their actions and desires in a brief moment in time. These words—mottos—were then formally infused into ships through ceremony and tradition and continue across time and space to inspire, motivate, and rally U.S. Navy sailors today. They hold special meaning for sailors who have had the good fortune to live by them. The truth captured in these simple mottos is passed on to each generation of sailors who walk up the brow of their ships, salute, and commit to serve their nation, navy, and shipmates.

We Stick Together holds special meaning for those of us fortunate to serve in USS THE SULLIVANS (DD-537) or (DDG-68). *We Stick Together* reflects the fighting spirit of five brothers from Waterloo and also what all families, crews, and nations should do, especially in the darkest hours and hardest times. For me, *We Stick Together* is a corrolary to *E Pluribus Unum* and represents the United States and how we should all act going forward in time.

Our armed forces each has their own mottos. The U.S. Navy's official motto is "Semper Fortis" (Always Strong). The United States Coast Guard's motto is "Semper Paratus" (Always Ready), and the United States Marine Corps' motto is famously claimed to be "Semper Fidelis" (Always Faithful). The U.S. Army and U.S. Air Force chose to go with English vice Latin mottos: "This We'll Defend" for the Army and "Aim High … Fly, Fight, Win" for the Air Force. The new U.S. Space Force chose "Semper Supra" for its motto, which translates in English as "Always Above." The mottos of our armed forces serve as concise mission statements. They provide a short executive summary to justify the hundreds of billions of dollars taxpayers pay for them. The language, Latin or English, that is used is not important, but the words do matter, especially if they are believed, followed, and acted upon by those who take an oath to serve.

Mottos do matter; and we should all reflect on which ones impact our actions and lives. Mottos are not merely buzzwords, advertising jingles, or passing fads; they have deep and lasting meaning for all of us who choose to serve something greater than self. Mottos encapsulate an institution's foundational goals, beliefs, and principles. Mottos are used by monarchs, dictators, and presidents for both good and evil. Mottos infuse life and personality into non-living things, such as a ship. They remind us of our purpose and mission, and they bind us together in duty and spirit.

Of all the mottos, good and bad, that I have ever heard, uttered, or thought about, *We Stick Together* has had the deepest impact and most meaning in my life. I would hear these words in my sleep and see them embedded in our correspondence and embroidered on our ball caps. This phrase became a mantra and motivating force, and would become deeply rooted in my subconscious mind in just one week aboard USS THE SULLIVANS (DDG-68). Reality also kicked in after a few days at sea. The story of the five brothers, the motto of this ship, and my journey to command all faded into the back of my mind as I grappled with the scope of the work that lay ahead. USS THE SULLIVANS (DDG-68) was en route to Scotland for a major advanced-phase multi-national exercise that would test our collective level of knowledge, tactical acumen, and overall effectiveness as a warship. I knew it would be a challenge and still did not really know the talents and weaknesses of this crew. We would soon find out how well our *We Stick Together* motto and spirit translated into warfighting prowess.

CHAPTER 5

SNOT BUBBLES AND A RING OF FIRE

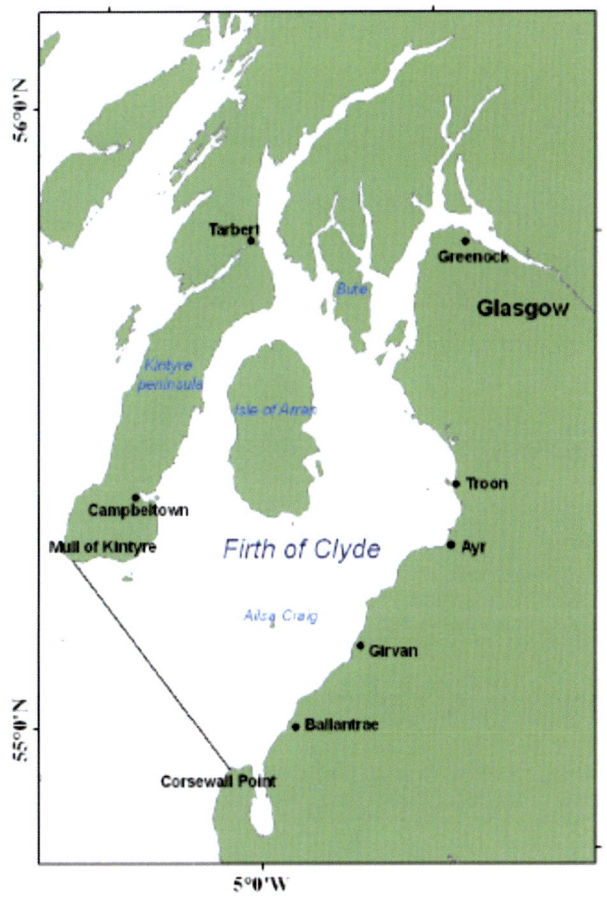

Map of Firth of Cylde, Scotland

CG-61, DDG-68, and FFG-28 conducting DIVTACs in 2006

On June 11, 2006 USS THE SULLIVANS (DDG-68) was steaming across the Atlantic Ocean in company with USS BOONE (FFG-28), a Mayport based Oliver Hazard Perry-class fast frigate, and USS MONTEREY (CG-61), an Aegis cruiser homeported in Norfolk, VA. THE SULLIVANS, BOONE, and MONTEREY were all headed to the Royal Navy's Clyde base in Faslane, Scotland, to conduct Exercise Neptune Warrior (NW 062). Neptune Warrior (now known as Joint Warrior) was a major multi-national military exercise organized and run by the Royal Navy, which took place every other year off the coast of Scotland in the Firth of Clyde. This exercise was a varsity-level event that pitted groups of ships under the banners of the fictional nations of Brownlandia and Mustardia. The two-week intense exercise was umpired by a senior Royal Navy admiral ashore in Faslane.

Preparations for Neptune Warrior are extensive and require weeks of special training and focus on NATO message writing, communications, and serialized exercises. In 2006 Neptune Warrior would include multi-warfare (air, undersea, surface) training evolutions, free play periods, and live fire events. The U.S. Navy used this exercise as advanced phase training to get ships ready for overseas deployments. Neptune Warrior 062 was USS THE SULLIVANS' (DDG-68) advance-phased training event for the upcoming six month deployment to the Mediterranean and Black Seas.

I had participated in Neptune Warrior once before in 1996 as a department head and tactical action officer (TAO) and remembered it being challenging. The Royal Navy always seemed three steps ahead of us when it came to succinct radio communications and coordination. This year's exercise would be no different. I had been in command all of six days and was trying to read and understand all the scheduled events. My learning curve and that of our wardroom, all of whom had never participated in a Neptune Warrior, was steep. We were drinking from a fire hose as we made our way across the Atlantic.

USS MONTEREY (CG-61) was the senior ship in our flotilla and had embarked our commodore, who was the officer in tactical control of all three ships as we crossed the Atlantic. On June 11, 2006, MONTEREY, BOONE, and THE SULLIVANS conducted division tactics (aka DIVTACs). DIVTACs are like marching for ships. They consist of synchronized turns and maneuvers in tight formations that are supposed to be smartly executed and precisely done. When done correctly, the timing and choreography should be uniform and sharp; think synchronized swimming or ballroom dancing for warships. Division tactics were used in both world wars to escort convoys, combat U-boats, and protect aircraft carriers from enemy aircraft attack. In ancient Rome, centurions would shout commands and the Roman legion would form up with their shields and swords in unison to counter the enemy. DIVTACs were the modern naval equivalent, but now used gas turbine engines and controllable, reversible pitch propellers to get into exact formations.

As a young junior officer who learned the surface warfare profession during the Cold War, DIVTACs served as the foundation for tactical ship handling. Cruisers, destroyers, and frigates would form a ring of steel around the aircraft carrier, which carried the admiral, the battle group staff, and dozens of fighters, bombers, and reconnaissance aircraft. The battle group was the center-piece of American superpower, and the U.S. Navy kept them deployed and on call as the world's gendarmerie. DIVTACs are supposed to be the bread and butter of U.S. Navy surface warriors, but on this day, USS THE SULLIVANS (DDG-68) was a soup sandwich, which is polite military jargon for FUBAR (f'd up beyond all recognition).

I distinctly remember being on the bridge and hearing the radio crackle with the command to immediate execute the given turn, but our bridge team did not respond nor maneuver. Suffice to say my expectations of their level of ship handling tactical prowess were not met. Both the conning officer and the officer of the deck had a glazed look in their eyes and were not anticipating when to turn or where to go. They were lost and USS THE SULLIVANS (DDG-68) was out of step and falling behind. The key to DIVTACs is to quickly figure out which ship is to be the guide of the formation and where that ship should be when we finish a given maneuver. The conning officer needed to know exactly how many yards and at what bearing from the guide our ship was supposed to be. When the signal was executed, the ship should accelerate at least five knots faster than base speed and take station as soon as possible. These signals were to be executed rapidly and precisely. Ships, crews, and captains were judged on how they performed DIVTACs. Once on station, we would report "alpha station," meaning we were in place and ready for action or the next signal. This whole process seemed to be a mystery to the USS THE SULLIVANS junior officers on watch that day. They did not have the same shared mental model I had. My honeymoon was over.

I watched as we drifted out of position. I knew where we had to go, but it seemed no one else did. I remember standing up and shouting something to the effect, "you are making us look stupid, like a second grader with snot bubbles running down their face. Get your shi$ together and figure out when on station what the guide should bare!" I was agitated and angry. This got their immediate attention. I took a breath and calmed down and then together we figured out where we needed to go. We finished the DIVTACs, but it was not pretty. We had not done well. We were all out of practice and needed to improve quickly if we wanted to keep pace with our Royal Navy friends in a couple of days' time.

Here is my entry in my Captain's journal the next day, June 12, 2006:

> Last two days have been good but problematic. Leapfrogs / DIVTACs yesterday was a soup sandwich. We got an interrogative station [radio call] and it blew us up. BOONE had a hard time too...

The lesson learned here was that I needed to provide my expectations to our ship drivers and show them what right looked like. They did not grow up in the Cold War and have dozens and dozens of DIVTAC events under their belts. I knew where we were supposed to be and that we had to think two steps ahead. We needed to work together and communicate the same shared mental model of THE SULLIVANS accelerating and turning sharply with 15 degrees of rudder to take station on the guide. It was my duty to teach them. In the moment and under stress, captains, especially those that have been in command for six days, forget why junior officers are called junior. I needed to remain calm and carry on as our British colleagues are so famous for doing. There would be no more snot bubble DIVTACs. We would get better and use each exercise and event to improve. That is why we were here. It was about raising our collective level of knowledge and improving teamwork. *We Stick Together* through snot bubbles and all.

Neptune Warrior 062 proved to be both challenging and rewarding. Establishing clear radio communications with our foreign partners was difficult at first but improved over time. USS THE SULLIVANS (DDG-68) received an incredible level of training in a short two weeks at sea. The Royal Navy has been at this for many centuries, and had no qualms showing their American cousins what right looks like. Getting our egos bruised a bit over the radio by proper British accents was a small price to pay to learn how to fight and win at sea. That is how you learn.

On June 15, 2006, USS THE SULLIVANS (DDG-68) arrived in Faslane and tied up outboard of USS BOONE (FFG-28). We spent a few days in port getting ready for two weeks of intense training at sea. We were still drinking from the firehose with regard to our learning curve and planning efforts. Like a football coach two weeks into training camp, I was beginning to see the talent we had in our wardroom, chief's mess, and mess decks. We had depth on the bench too, but all needed practice and polishing. Neptune Warrior 062 was going to be the very challenge we needed to improve.

On day one of Neptune Warrior, June 19, 2006, as USS THE SULLIVANS (DDG-68) was leaving port, Royal Navy fast attack craft and jet skis ambushed us as we slowly headed out of the harbor. This is exactly how the Iranians, North Koreans, and Al-Qaeda were preparing to take out U.S. warships. It is an old trick and one the fledgling American Navy used against the British effectively in our revolution. It still worked in 2006, especially when watch standers were not ready. The learning had just begun.

From June 19-30, 2006, USS THE SULLIVANS (DDG-68) faced air raids, mine fields, submarines, and enemy surface combatants while steaming close to shore in the inclement Scottish weather of the Firth of Clyde. We partnered with Spanish, Turkish, French, and other NATO ships supporting the mythical land of Mustardia. And like Jonathan Swift's satirical Liliputians in *Gulliver's Travels*, we battled with our foes, who were made up of other U.S., British, and NATO ships, in pursuit of ridiculous make-believe national interests. Some of USS THE SULLIVANS (DDG-68) officers really got into the role playing of the Mustardians, creating a flag and a crest and even composing a Mustardian national anthem that they would hum while on watch. In the end it did not matter whether the Mustardians defeated the Brownlandians or the other way around. What mattered most on this two-week journey along the cold rocky coast of Scotland was the hard-won lessons learned from mock battles between teams of young men and women in all the ships, submarines, and aircraft.

Some of the more memorable training events included another at sea ambush, this time by Swedish and German patrol boats; completing an underway replenishment with RFA FT AUSTIN (A-386); tracking the British submarine HMS TURBULENT (S-87) with sonar; and conducting a live five-inch gunnery exercise off Cape Wrath, Scotland. Neptune Warrior was a varsity-level cornucopia of intensity that our sailors needed. They had been through the gauntlet and survived. Their reward for all this hard work would be a couple of port visits in Europe before heading back to Mayport. Upon completion of Neptune Warrior, USS BOONE (FFG-28), USS MONTEREY (CG-61) and USS THE SULLIVANS (DDG-68) parted ways and headed to their respective port visits in Northwestern Europe. USS THE SULLIVANS (DDG-68) would visit Aarhus, Denmark, and Cobh, Ireland.

Map of Denmark depicting USS THE SULLIVANS' track into Aarhus in 2006

USS THE SULLIVANS (DDG-68) left Scotland on June 30, 2006. We were headed to Aarhus for a port call and to celebrate the Fourth of July. Before we passed through the busy Skagerrak–Kattegat Straits, we still had work to do. Here is what I entered in my journal for that day:

Captain's Journal entry, 30 June 2006:

At sea [in] North Sea 1 day out of Aarhus, Denmark, speed 20.2
knots, trail shaft, course 119 true. Neptune Warrior 062 [hostilities
officially] ended yesterday in the Southern Minches. We killed
some Norwegian patrol boats, Brown[landian] helos, and USS
MONTEREY (CG-61) along with the Spanish frigate SNS ALVARO
DE BAZAN (F-100). Following the encounter [,] we unrepped
[conducted an underway replenishment at sea] with RFA OAKLEAF
(A-111). A little hairy when a stubborn Scottish fisherman didn't
seem to want to move out of the way. After taking 81,000 gallons
of DFM [diesel fuel marine] we set flight quarters and landed SNS
PATIÑO's (A-14) Gato 5, a UH-1 Huey [helicopter], to transport
5 pax [passengers]. Following that we raced SNS ALVARO DE
BAZAN (F-100), exchanged pleasantries on VHF B to B [bridge to
bridge radio] and headed north. A lot went wrong [during Neptune
Warrior 062] but more went right …

USS THE SULLIVANS (DDG-68) arrived in Aarhus on Saturday, July 1, 2006. Aarhus is a picturesque Danish city located on the eastern coast of Jutland, 116 miles northwest of the capital, Copenhagen. The crew was granted overnight liberty and behaved well. USS THE SULLIVANS (DDG-68) hosted the Danish Chief of Naval Operations, the U.S. ambassador to Denmark, and participated in the largest Fourth of July celebration held annually outside the United States, which is near Aalborg, Denmark. Prior to attending this overseas Fourth of July celebration, no one onboard our ship had any idea or could have guessed that the Danes were America's biggest fans. The learning never stopped in USS THE SULLIVANS (DDG-68).

Marselisborg Palace, residence of Danish Royal family in Aarhus, Denmark

One memorable and humorous incident occurred on the grounds of the Marselisborg Palace, the summer home of the Danish royal family and Margrethe II, Queen of Denmark. Many USS THE SULLIVANS (DDG-68) sailors loved playing two-hand touch football on their off days. Marselisborg Palace had beautiful grounds and hundreds of yards of green grass that was not fenced in. It also happened to be located a short walking distance from the pier where we were moored in Aarhus. On a beautiful summer afternoon at the royal palace, the local inhabitants of Aarhus, along with the Queen's family, got free box seats to a serious THE SULLIVANS two hand touch football smack down. "Hut, hut … one Mississippi, two Mississippi, three Mississippi." Audibles, plays, and shouts echoed off the royal palace. There were white-striped Wilson NCAA collegiate footballs flying through the air; it was an American extravaganza and on par with the excellent 2005 12-4 season our hometown Jacksonville Jaguars had finished with. THE SULLIVANS sailors played this pick-up game with as much passion and focus as the NFL stars they admired.

Our sailors had no idea whose house this was or that its grounds were not designated for sports. The Danes seemed to enjoy biking, jogging, and having fun outside everywhere in Aarhus. There were designated bicycle lanes adjacent to most streets marked clearly with signs. However, around the Marselisborg Palace there were no visible signs or warning placards that told people to keep off the grass or warning of prosecutions for those who trespass on the Queen's lawn. The scenic and well manicured grounds looked like a city park to American sailors. Our crew played and many locals gathered and watched in amazement, not because of our sailors' NFL-like skills but because of where they chose to play-at the Queen's house. No one stopped them and no one would have known had not our Danish military liaison mentioned it to me. He was smiling and not upset. I believe the Queen forgave us this trespass. I am sure George, Francis, Joseph, Madison, and Albert would have joined in if they could. They were certainly there in spirit. It was easy to imagine them playing football with our crew, running passing routes and diving for throws to an imaginary sideline.

Swedish Coast Guard patrol vessel

Abba LPs from 1970s and 1980s

On July 5, 2006, USS THE SULLIVANS (DDG-68) was underway from Aarhus and bound for Cobh. As we departed, a Swedish patrol ship queried us and stated that we had violated their territorial waters. USS THE SULLIVANS (DDG-68) was conducting innocent passage at a moderate speed along our planned track. We thought nothing of this hail and accusation by the neutral Swedes, makers of Volvos, Ikea furniture, and the 70s band Abba. We logged the radio call and moved on towards our destination in Ireland. Only much later did it dawn on me that the Swedes were the descendants of the Vikings. I found out the hard way that Swedish leaders had traded in their double-bladed battle axes for diplomatic demarches. Lesson learned, you do not want to be named in an official diplomatic demarche unless you enjoy Congressional inquiries, endless legal paperwork, and working closely with the U.S. Department of State.

In the end everything turned out okay and we did not go to war with Sweden or have to boycott Ikea. The Swedish Government apparently files demarches on all foreign warships transiting to and from Denmark because of a long-standing policy regarding their claimed territorial waters. It would have been nice to know this before we conducted our voyage planning but we were unaware. The lesson learned here was that we needed to do our own research and homework for all our future overseas port visits to prevent political and physical damage from impacting USS THE SULLIVANS (DDG-68).

As fate and karma would have it, from 2012 to 2015, I would serve as the Senior Defense Official, Defense Attaché (SDO DATT) to Italy. I would become intimately familiar with diplomatic demarches and work for and with the U.S. Department of State. I would also become good friends with the Swedish military attaché, and learn the importance of using demarches in international law and modern diplomacy. Everything happens for a reason, which might not be immediately clear to us in the present, but becomes visible in time.

USS THE SULLIVANS (DDG-68) visited Cobh, Ireland
July 08-11, 2006-view of deep water quay

On July 8, 2006, USS THE SULLIVANS (DDG-68) arrived in Cobh (pronounced COVE) for a three-day port visit. Cobh is a scenic port town on the Southeast coast of Ireland. It serves as the main port for the city of Cork and was one of the last ports of call for the HMS *TITANIC* on her fateful voyage in April 1912. Our schedule in Cobh was not as busy as our previous port of call in Denmark. We would host one formal event onboard for the mayor and her staff and make some official calls on the Irish military. We all looked forward to relaxing a bit in the ancestral home of our namesakes.

The Sullivan family originally came from County Cork. USS THE SULLIVANS (DDG-68) had visited Ireland previously during the summer of 2003 to pay homage to the homeland of our fallen heroes. The story of the American Sullivan brothers was well known in Ireland. The people in Cobh let us know that they too could relate to sacrifice, pain, and loss. Some of the local towns people would remind us over a few pints that Ireland struggled for centuries to gain independence from Britain, and many suffered under their imperial yoke.

Although not Irish myself in anyway but spirit, I knew Irish pride ran deep from growing up near Boston and having many Irish Catholic friends. The Irish, like Sicilians, were proud of their past and sent millions of immigrants to America in the early twentieth century. In Gloucester where I grew up, many families would display the Irish green, white, and orange flag next to the American flag over or near the front entrance to their colonial salt-box or tudor-style wooden homes. Italian families would do the same with the green, white, and red Italian tricolor. In the summer sun in New England, the orange and red colors of both flags would fade out, making Irish-American and Italian-American houses indistinguishable from one another. While some of the Irish or Sicilian grandparents who lived in these homes might speak in Gaelic or Sicilian dialect when they didn't want their children to know what they were saying, most of us kids spoke the same Boston-accented English, dropping r's from the end of words and adding them where they didn't belong. Lobster would become lobstah and Maria would sound like Maria-er. Irish and Sicilian families would transform in one generation from the ways of the old world to the new. It didn't matter if your home had an Irish or Italian flag over it as long as the Red Sox beat the Yankees and Patriots, Celtics, and Bruins won. In Gloucester, the American melting pot was real, but looked, smelled, tasted, and sounded like New England clam chowdah.

I always felt a kindred spirit with my Irish-American friends. Ireland, like Sicily, was an island nation that suffered many invasions and developed its own unique culture and language over the centuries. Many Irish and Sicilians immigrated to America with nothing and worked extremely hard to give their families more than they ever dreamed of having, most importantly a chance to be free and pursue happiness. In the late nineteenth and early twentieth centuries, Irish and Sicilian American families tended to be large and close-knit and clung devoutly to their Roman Catholic faith. Ireland and Sicily have their dark sides too.

Irish patriotism was marred by the terrorism of the Irish Republican Army (IRA) and other offshoot groups, while Sicilian-Americans were all lumped together with *La Cosa Nostra* (aka the Mafia), as made famous by Francis Ford Coppola's *The Godfather* movie trilogy. The truth was that the overwhelming majority of Irish and Sicilian Americans have nothing to do with either the IRA or the Mafia. These violent groups do not represent the contribution that millions of Irish and Sicilian Americans have made to the United States, the U.S. Navy, or USS THE SULLIVANS (DDG-68). *We Stick Together* did not romanticize or celebrate terrorism, crime, and lawlessness, but was centered on truth, justice, and the American way.

We Stick Together translates as *bataimid le chéile* in Irish Gaelic, but during our visit to Cobh, we found it needed no translation. Cobh was my first visit to Ireland, and it wildly exceeded my expectations. It is a beautiful place inhabited by sharp-witted people who enjoy a deep laugh, the kind that makes you cry. I also found that some of the inhabitants of Cobh enjoyed baptizing new friendships with locally crafted libations. George, Francis, Joseph, Madison, and Albert Sullivan were probably much the same in spirit and attitude as their kin who lived close by in County Cork in the province of Munster, an area known for its famous rebels, most notably Michael Collins, the dashing Irish revolutionary and political leader of the Irish Free State who was assassinated in 1922 near Cork. He was portrayed by Liam Neeson in the 1996 biographical film *Michael Collins*.

During our stay in Cobh I learned that my mental model of Ireland and Irish culture was flawed. Movies like *Michael Collins* merged with 30-second TV commercials of Irish Spring soap and Lucky Charms breakfast cereal to form an unrealistic melange of the Ireland I thought I knew . Drinking green beer during St. Patrick's Day parades in Boston and Newport was not reflective of real Irish culture any more so than the caricatures of leprechauns embroidered on Boston Celtic jerseys and Notre Dame sweatshirts. I must admit that while I did find the food and drink around Cobh to be "magically delicious," I did not know as much as I previously thought about Ireland and the Irish people. This blissful and well-intentioned ignorance would end in a ring of fire as I became the protagonist in my own Irish limerick.

There once was a ship named THE SULLIVANS
that came to Cobh to have a little fun again

The ship's captain made a bet
of which he did not regret

An old tune and some lasses
Caused some citizens to harass us

So the ship left in a Ring of Fire
Because the captain was no liar

The lesson learned is you can't please everyone
Even on a warship with shamrocks and a five-inch gun

On our last full day in Cobh, and after completing my official duties, I walked down the brow and across the street to a pub, which had a large banner that read, "Welcome USS THE SULLIVANS (DDG-68)." I walked up to the bar and ordered a pint of Guinness. The barkeep frowned and looked at me as if I were stupid. He told me, "Son, you can't get Guinness in here only Murphy's."

Once again my knowledge of the Celts and Ireland failed me. Murphy's Irish Stout was brewed in Cork and the dominant ale in Cobh. Guinness was brewed in Dublin and served there and in the surrounding areas. Lesson learned: when in pubs in Cork or Cobh, order Murphy's Irish stout, not Guinness.

As I was not a big fan of dark beer anyway, it made no difference to me, so Murphy's it was. As I sipped the dark ale, a fellow pub patron, who had overheard my faux pas, and was downing his own pint of Murphy's a few stools down the bar from me came over and introduced himself as Sean. Sean said he was a boat builder and really liked the look of USS THE SULLIVANS (DDG-68). He worked in wood but appreciated the rake of the hull, symmetry, and angled mast and deck house. He asked if I was a sailor from the ship. I thought of dropping the song lyric from Richie Valen's "La Bamba" on him, "yo no soy marinero, soy capitan, soy capitan," but instead I just replied that I was the captain of the ship. Sean laughed and told me to F ... off and some other choice words in Gaelic which I could not understand. I repeated I am the captain of USS THE SULLIVANS (DDG-68). He still did not believe me. I am not sure why. Perhaps it was because sea captains in Ireland were old and grizzled and not 39 and beardless like me. Sean had downed a few pints of Murphy's by now. He muttered, "If you are the G ... damn captain of that ship I want you to play Johnny Cash's "Ring of Fire" when you leave port, and I want to come onboard and take a picture with two of the prettiest lasses in your crew, preferably officers." I thought that a bizarre demand, but I humored him. "You're on," I said. "I can make that happen." "Caic tarbh!" he said, which loosely translates to "bullsh#%" in standard American English.

Sean and I continued to talk. I quite enjoyed his perspective on life in Cobh and Irish politics as well as his profanity-laced Gaelic lessons. Sean explained that in school, Irish kids are forced to learn Gaelic and speak Gaelic, but the vast majority hate it and never use it. It is a difficult language to learn with very few proficient speakers in a country of just over four million. No one anywhere else in the world uses Irish Gaelic except on St. Patrick's Day. Sean said for reasons he could not explain he always liked Gaelic and enjoyed its challenging grammar and the old ways of the Irish. Perhaps that is why he made wooden boats. I shook Sean's hand and told him that as captain of USS THE SULLIVANS (DDG-68) I was formally inviting him to our VIP reception for the mayor and other dignitaries of the Irish Republic that evening. I told him the Irish Chief of Naval Operations (CNO) would be there, and that it would be a good networking opportunity for him. Sean reluctantly agreed to come aboard. I do not believe that he thought I was actually the captain of the ship, more like a crew member pulling his leg. He agreed to come nevertheless.

That night USS THE SULLIVANS (DDG-68) hosted a flight deck reception and provided tours for the dignitaries of Cobh and Cork. I gave a short speech to the crowd and explained how our crew really took our motto, *We Stick Together*, to heart. I explained why we had a giant set of shamrocks in green on our stack and why the name THE SULLIVANS was painted in green on the stern sheet. The visitors listened and understood, but from their body language I got the sense that our European cousins viewed us as being over-the-top-cheeky, and the cosmetic flair of our ship was just a bit much for them. I thought maybe it was my delivery. I was genuinely enthused about bringing the U.S. Navy's most Irish ship to Ireland. I supposed my audience, being actually Irish, did not need giant shamrocks and green paint to know who they were.

After my short speech and handshakes with our guests, I spotted Sean on the flight deck. He had come after all. I saw him arm in arm with two of our female junior officers. His grin said it all. He smiled and we exchanged slàinte *(pronounced SLAANT–CHA)* and we drank a toast to friendship and honesty. Sean could not deny that I was the captain, but he probably knew all along. I watched as he posed for photos with our sailors, especially our female sailors. It was all in good fun, but I had kept my word and intended on keeping the rest of my promise to him.

I saw the Irish CNO standing nearby, so I walked up and introduced myself and said hello. We exchanged pleasantries and hit it off. The admiral then half joked in a crisp brogue, "Can we have the ship after you're done with her, as you already have her painted nicely?" I let him know that USS THE SULLIVANS had many more years of service left in her, and that after that she would likely become a floating museum like her predecessor in Buffalo. In 2006, the Irish Navy consisted of a few offshore patrol vessels and some patrol boats. It might have had 1,500 personnel total. I think the Irish CNO really would have taken any ship the U.S. Navy would offer. The night went on and our visit to Ireland was coming to an end. It had gone well, and everyone in our crew was glad they got to see where George, Francis, Joseph, Madison, and Albert's family came from. It provided another aspect to their story and would stay with us forever.

The next morning at 0715 USS THE SULLIVANS (DDG-68) got under-way from Cobh. I had our officer of the deck plug in her iPod and play Johnny Cash's "Ring of Fire" as loud as it would go and still sound audi-ble. Our sailors on the forecastle and fantail looked confused. Normally we only played music on the 1MC topside when we broke away during an underway replenishment. Johnny Cash was not unfamiliar to them, but "Ring of Fire" seemed an odd choice for so early in the morning. I had kept my word to Sean. It felt good to hear the man in black belting out "Ring of Fire" as we pulled away from Cobh.

Local anti-war activists in Cobh had heard the music too. They would write an online story claiming that USS THE SULLIVANS (DDG-68) delib-erately played this song to wake the residents of Cobh up:

"Many Cobh residents woke to the strains of Johnny Cash belting out his 1960s hit "Ring of Fire" over the public address system of USS The Sullivans as she left the Deepwater Quay in Cobh this morning (Tuesday, 11/7/06) around 7.15 after her eventful weekend in Cork Harbour.

Last night less than half of the reported 50 invited local worthies turned up. Many of those were visibly embarrassed at having to pass anti-war protesters. Only four of the nine members of Cobh Town Council were seen going aboard ship... Also going to last night's reception were senior members of the Irish Naval Service (a neutral country?) and top brass from the semi-state Port of Cork company. Senior local authority and tourism figures were also in attendance. Two of the ship's company operated a stall selling souvenirs from the USS [Sullivan] including sweatshirts (from sweatshops no doubt), pens, zippo lighters and the mandatory baseball caps. Prices were displayed in Euros with 25 Euro being the price of a sweatshirt. Only two or three souvenirs were sold and by 7pm the stallholders closed up shop. Some of the worthies from the Irish navy and council were seen leaving later with similar trophies. I took some photographs of the stall and one of the US stall operators repeatedly ordered me to stop taking his photograph. I refused and he then told me to "get out of here", I reminded him that I was a resident of Cobh and a citizen of Ireland and that he should get out of here, taking his ship with him.[14"]

Later our crew would learn that there were some Irish citizens who were not happy with the U.S. military using the airport at Shannon, Ireland, as a stop over point for troops and equipment headed to Iraq for the U.S. war effort there. Some Irish citizens felt that it violated their nation's neutrality. While the vast majority of citizens in Cobh seemed glad to host USS THE SULLIVANS (DDG-68) in their quaint seaside town, a minority were clearly angered by our arrival, and even more upset with their local leaders and government officials for coming to our ship for a friendly reception. In Cobh we had seen only a handful of people protesting our arrival and never gave it much thought. The lesson learned here was that we needed to know the political context of the ports we were going to visit in the future. This would be especially important on our deployment to the Mediterranean and Black Seas.

Truth is often stranger than fiction. Following through on a simple pub challenge over a pint of Murphy's Irish stout and playing an old Johnny Cash tune over the 1MC was misconstrued (or purposely twisted) as a political act by Irish anti-war protesters with an axe to grind. I was unaware of the political machinations of County Cork and Cobh. I kept my word to Sean and would do the same again. There were many lessons learned

---

14 http://www.indymedia.ie/article/77162?userlanguage=ga&save_prefs=true dated July 11, 2006.

during our visit to Cobh. I learned that my level of knowledge about Ireland and Irish culture was low. I realized my low fuel gas tank light was on culturally speaking when I ordered a pint of Guinness instead of Murphy's in Cobh. Our crew also learned that you cannot please everyone all the time. Souvenir stands, receptions, and even Johnny Cash could be interpreted as hostile imperialism by some. *We Stick Together* meant maintaining your word and keeping your character strong even in the face of unexpected adversity. Slàinte!

Our transit back across the Atlantic was pleasant and relatively uneventful with the exception of a medical evacuation (medivac) flight for a chief who got his hand slammed in a water-tight door. Five or six hours after we left Cobh the seas picked up a bit. Our smoking area was located in a spot we called the port break. It was situated on the main deck just aft of the forecastle and provided shelter from the wind but did not allow smoke to enter the ship. One of our chiefs was taking a smoke break when a wave impacted the ship and the heavy water tight door leading into the port break slammed against his hand, producing a nasty cut and exposing ligaments and tendons. Luckily we were able to notify the Irish Coast Guard who provided a helicopter to to airlift him off the ship and get him to a specialist to repair his hand. Had this accident happened farther out to sea, the chief might have lost the use of his hand as he needed surgery to repair damaged ligaments. Smoking proved to be an unhealthy habit, especially in the North Atlantic.

Our next trip across the Atlantic would be in less than five months. This time we would pass between the Pillars of Hercules (i.e., the Strait of Gibraltar) and enter the Mediterranean Sea for a six month deployment in support of the Global War on Terror (GWOT), European Command (EUCOM), and Naval Forces Europe. More mystery and adventures awaited us. We had learned many valuable lessons that would help us on this next voyage. We would also visit ancient and mysterious lands that would leave us all in awe and wonder.

CHAPTER 6

I Want to Believe ... Known Unknowns

USS THE SULLIVANS (DDG-68) at dusk 2006 near La Maddalena, Sardinia

USS THE SULLIVANS (DDG-68) search and rescue swimmer training 2007

Do you believe in UFOs? How about UAP (unidentified aerial phenomena)? I for one have always been both skeptical and fascinated by the possibility that aliens from another world or dimension could be visiting us now or have in the past. The popularity of TV programs such as *The X-files* and the History Channel's long-running series *Ancient Aliens* speak to the millions of people who want to believe. I will admit when I can find nothing else to watch on television, I sometimes settle on an episode of *Ancient Aliens*, keeping my mind open but my windows and curtains closed. Some of the premises in these episodes are so outlandish and illogical, but they are presented with such conviction and clarity that many of our fellow citizens believe there has been a U.S. Government cover up regarding UFOs since the 1947 Roswell incident.

While I am not sure if aliens exist, I am sure that incompetence, miscommunication, and a general lack of knowledge run deep in all government bureaucracies. Could the U.S. Government pull off a massive conspiracy about UFOs for over 75 years? That would be an incredible achievement. Unfortunately, and more likely, our leaders are often confused about what is true and what is not. This was best exemplified by Secretary of Defense, Donald Rumsfeld during a press conference in 2002 in the lead up to what would become Operation Iraqi Freedom, when he famously stated:

As we know, there are known knowns; there are things we know we know. We also know there are known unknowns; that is to say we know there are some things we do not know. But there are also unknown unknowns—the ones we don't know we don't know.[15]

In December 2006, USS THE SULLIVANS (DDG-68) had a known unknown incident occur. Our ship encountered and tracked three inexplicable strange lights high in the night sky while we were crossing the Atlantic Ocean. The incident was never officially reported or documented that I am aware. I am not sure if others in our crew told loved ones what they encountered when they returned from sea. I never have until today. I kept the following story hidden in my captain's journal for many years, but now feel I can speak about it.

For the record, I have been a big fan of *Coast to Coast* AM since 1993. For those who are not familiar with *Coast to Coast*, it is a national radio

---

15 https://www.theatlantic.com/politics/archive/2014/03/rumsfelds-knowns-and-unknowns-the-intellectual-history-of-a-quip/359719/ David A. Graham, "Rumsfeld's Knowns and Unknowns: The Intellectual History of a Quip," The Atlantic, March 28, 2014.

program, usually on AM stations that broadcasts from late in the evening to the early morning hours. Millions of Americans listen to *Coast to Coast*, which focuses on topics that the main-stream media would consider strange or even kooky. UFOs, aliens, bigfoot, paranormal phenomena, and the afterlife are the mainstay of this long running program, but many other mainstream topics are discussed for hour-long segments as well. For me, the show falls somewhere between Joe Rogan's podcast and CBS's *60 minutes*. It is an interesting family-friendly radio show that is well done. Probably the most appealing aspect of *Coast to Coast* for me is that the current host, Mr. George Noory, is a U.S. Navy veteran, who is honest, open, and patient with both callers and guests. He is professional and never take sides politically, while remaining open to people of all educational levels. He genuinely wants to help people, and is especially fond of working-class Americans: just my kind of guy.

I have always kept an open mind but was never a fervent believer in UFOs, flying saucers, or aliens. This was especially true when I was in command of U.S. warships. However, several months back Mr. George Noory and his team at *Coast to Coast* reported what appeared to me to be the most credible evidence I had ever heard of actual proof of a UFO encounter by U.S. Navy pilots flying from the deck of USS NIMITZ (CVN-68). This report triggered my memory about the incident we witnessed one night on board USS THE SULLIVANS (DDG-68) back in 2006.

On the night of December 3, 2006, while crossing the North Atlantic aboard USS THE SULLIVANS (DDG-68) we saw and tracked three bright objects in the night sky. Our ship was transiting at 16 knots in the mid-North Atlantic on a great circle route headed towards the Strait of Gibraltar and the U.S. Navy's Sixth Fleet area of operations (Mediterranean and Black Seas) for a six-month deployment in support of what was then known as GWOT. We had been at sea for seven days after departing our homeport of Mayport on November 27, 2006. We were sailing in company with USS KAUFFMAN (FFG-59), an Oliver Hazard Perry-class frigate out of Norfolk.

I remember being on the bridge that night after a leisurely Sunday at sea. As the captain I was required to write night orders, sign them, and then ensure that the required watch standers read and followed them. I was on the bridge dropping off these orders and took a moment to admire the beautiful clear skies when we noticed three distinct white lights in the sky ahead of the ship. I remember the lights looked out of place and lower in the sky than the background stars. There were no commercial airplanes or ships in our vicinity in this part of the Atlantic that night. USS KAUFFMAN (FFG-59) was sailing in company with us but was not within visual range of our ship. It was a beautiful clear, cool early December evening with a bright moon and lots of stars visible.

The bridge team and I noticed the lights at about the same time. The lights were round, whitish to yellow and very distinct. I remember they were in a triangular pattern. The lights were bright but not overwhelming. They were not aircraft warning lights nor were they stars. We all looked through binoculars and discussed what we thought these lights were. Some thought they could be satellites while I thought they could be high-altitude weather balloons. Now most of us had witnessed satellites at sea before, and I remember we distinctly ruled this out as a possibility because satellites often appeared much smaller and consisted of blinking—not steady—lights.

At the time I did not believe that the lights we were seeing were satellites, nor did I think they were stars. Both our quartermaster of the watch and navigator offered up the theory that what we were seeing was a reflection or refraction from a star in the upper atmosphere. He then went to his electronic star chart and said that the lights were in the vicinity of Sirius, the dog star, and what we must have been seeing was some sort of tri-refraction of Sirius.

Sirius, alpha canis majoris—the Dog Star and Orion's Belt (aka As Três Marias in Portuguese)

This made logical sense but did not appear to be correct because the three lights were brighter than any star, much lower in the sky than the other background stars, and seemed to be moving relative to our ship. The lights we were seeing were not part of Orion's Belt and appeared too clear to be refracted star images in my opinion. We were all stumped, yet kept trying to hypothesize what exactly we were seeing in the night sky hundreds of miles from the nearest land.

Aegis destroyers are equipped with the world's most sophisticated and powerful radar, the SPY-1D. The specific detection capabilities of the SPY-1D are classified, but suffice to say the radar is capable of detecting a golf ball size target at ranges in excess of 150 miles at almost any altitude. On the night in question, USS THE SULLIVANS (DDG-68) had solid SPY track on three objects at an altitude of 100,000 feet. The objects correlated to what we were seeing with our eyes on the bridge, but this made no sense. Neither commercial aircraft or low earth orbit satellites operate in this part of the stratosphere. Our quartermaster and navigator both believed what we were seeing was some sort of star light refraction, but refractions and reflections do not paint on radar and have distinct altitudes. I remember challenging our combat watchstanders and asking them if these were clutter tracks. They responded that they were sure we were tracking real objects at extremely high altitudes. I think they believed these tracks to be satellites or space junk, but this did not correlate to the lights we were seeing from the bridge.

Questioning attitude is a fundamental U.S. Navy operating principle. Sailors are taught, trained, and drilled on being mindful of their actions and questioning things that do not make sense. USS THE SULLIVANS (DDG-68) sailors were well trained and not shy about asking what right was supposed to look like. On the night of December 3, 2006, what we saw just did not make sense. We were all puzzled but kept hypothesizing and rationalizing what our eyes and sensors were telling us. It was a mystery that we just could not solve.

I remember we joked that perhaps aliens were tracking us as we crossed the Atlantic. Our bridge and combat Information teams worked on identifying these lights for quite awhile as I remember; something like 15 or 30 minutes until the lights simply disappeared. These lights did not move rapidly nor did they travel at a high velocity that I recall. I also do not remember what speed and course our Aegis combat system computed for their trajectory. I do recall distinctly that the altitude was 100,000 feet, which I thought was an odd thing at the time. In the end we never figured out what we were seeing or tracking that night in the middle of the Atlantic.

The following is an exact quote of what I wrote down the next day in my captain's journal:

04 Dec 06

Last night we thought we had three small air contacts. I thought they were weax balloons but Nav said it was Sirius, the Dog Star simply refracting in the light of the moon. The Spy techs swear they were tracking something... .spooky.

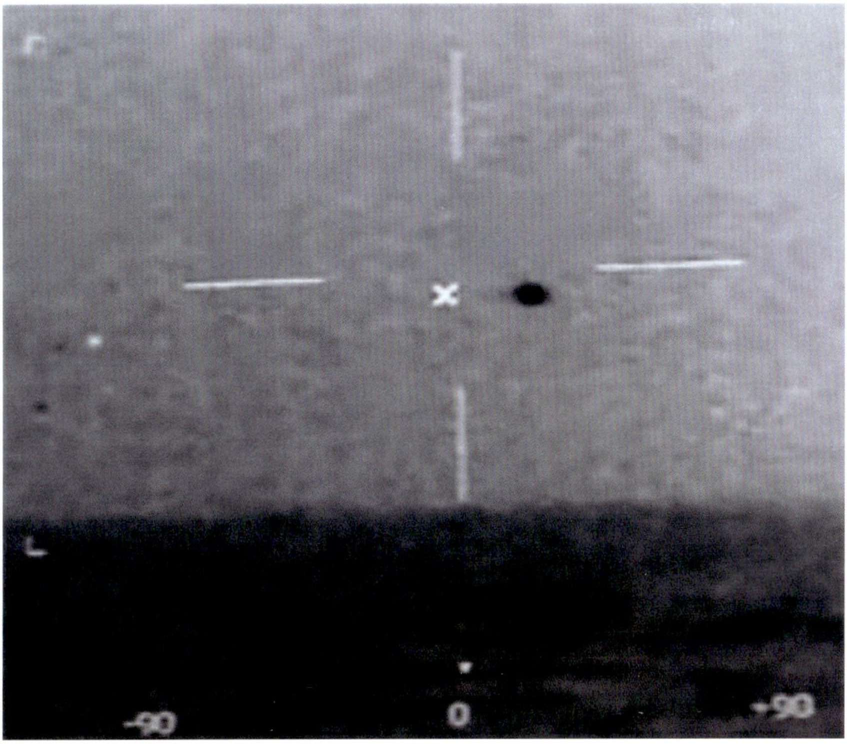

UAP Footage from USS OMAHA (LCS-12) July 2019

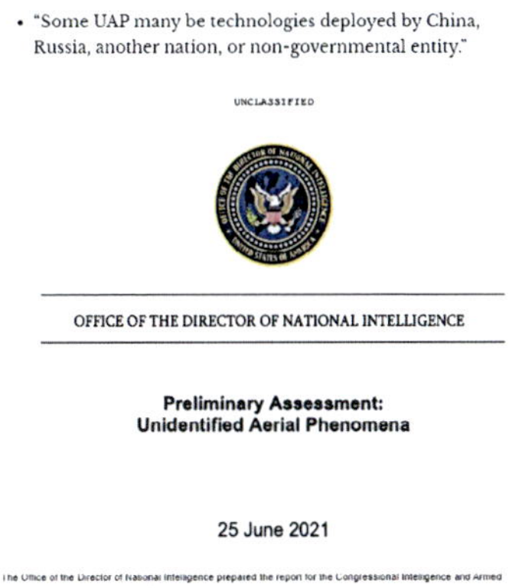

- "Some UAP many be technologies deployed by China, Russia, another nation, or non-governmental entity."

UNCLASSIFIED

OFFICE OF THE DIRECTOR OF NATIONAL INTELLIGENCE

Preliminary Assessment:
Unidentified Aerial Phenomena

25 June 2021

The Office of the Director of National Intelligence prepared the report for the Congressional Intelligence and Armed

U.S. Government report to Congress 2021 about UAP

To this day I am not sure what we saw and tracked that night. I only know that it happened. In hindsight, I wish we would have taken video or photographs of the lights, but we did not. I do remember that no one in the crew felt threatened or frightened about what we saw, only curious. Perhaps there are many similar sea stories waiting to be told. It is my hope that this true sea story will encourage more professional mariners and military personnel to come forward so that we can catalog these sightings and investigate them in a scientific manner. The U.S. Navy demands sailors have a questioning attitude and develop strong critical thinking skills in order to solve problems and win wars. This known unknown incident excited our professional curiosity and made us all wonder. We did not report it because we did not have enough information to report. We did not engage these contacts because there was no hostile intent or hostile act that we could detect. We only watched, discussed, and hypothesized. After the lights disappeared suddenly our professional curiosity diminished and we shifted focus to the known knowns in our schedule.

The lesson learned here is that strange things happen to mariners around the world. Most of their stories likely go unreported and they become known unknowns. Some of these stories are passed down and some maybe embellished. I can attest that this one happened, and it will be my known unknown from my time in command of USS THE SULLIVANS (DDG-68).

CHAPTER 7

CRITICAL THINKING AND THE PURSUIT OF TRUTH

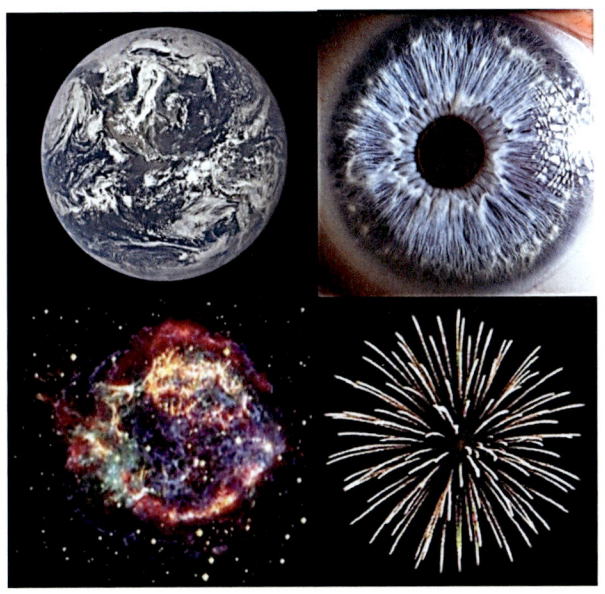

The earth, a human eye, nucleus of an atom, and an exploding firework

What do the earth, a human eye, the nucleus of an atom, and a firework all have in common? Besides being spherical, colorful, and beautiful, they all exist in nature and are shaped by the same fundamental physical forces that impact everything in the universe (i.e., gravity, electromagnetism, the strong force, and the weak force). Many believe that all things are made from "star dust," which came into existence sometime between 13 and 15 billion years ago, according to the Big Bang theory. The earth, the eye, the atomic nucleus, and the firework can also be studied, compared, analyzed, and understood through critical thinking.

According to www.criticalthinking.org, "Critical thinking is the intellectually disciplined process of actively and skillfully conceptualizing, applying, analyzing, synthesizing, and/or evaluating information gathered from, or generated by, observation, experience, reflection, reasoning, or communication, as a guide to belief and action."[16] Critical thinking can incorporate the scientific method, deductive reasoning, high-velocity learning, and myriad other techniques to improve one's perspective and understanding of the truth. In the U.S. Navy, critical thinking is a skill we want all our sailors to develop. The U.S. Navy trains, educates, and pushes all its sailors, from seaman to admiral, to be independent minded, think for themselves, and do the right thing, especially when no one is looking. Critical thinking and the pursuit of truth flow from the U.S. Navy value of honor and the fundamental operating principle of integrity.

In USS THE SULLIVANS (DDG-68) the critical thinking sailor was what our leadership triad—captain, executive officer, and command master chief—constantly emphasized. A smart, thinking sailor is an exponentially better mariner and warfighter. Critical thinking helps with crisis prevention and problem-solving. It also builds self-confidence and leadership ability. Critical thinking is more than just analyzing data and forging a testable hypothesis. In the U.S. Navy, and especially aboard USS THE

---

16 This specific quote was taken from this website https://www.criticalthinking.org/ circa 2016. The current website has a different design now and no longer lists this specific definition as of June 2021.

SULLIVANS (DDG-68), critical thinking was all about the pursuit of truth with an open, unbiased mind.

Ah, but what is truth? *Quid est veritas*? That is a profound, philosophical, and metaphysical question that brilliant minds have studied for millennia. Aristotle, St. Augustine, Albert Einstein, as well as the creators of the hit TV show *The X Files*, and many, many others have thought long and hard about this question. And while we all agree that the truth is out there, many people disagree on the best way to find it and what it actually means. The internet might have made searching for information easier, but it has also made finding the truth more difficult. Fake news and fact checkers are everywhere, but the truth still seems to elude many of us.

Dictionary.com defines "truth" as "the true or actual state of a matter-conformity with fact or reality; verity; a verified or indisputable fact, proposition, principle, or the like."[17] In Latin, the word for "truth" is "veritas." Latin-based languages use derivatives of this word: Spanish: verdad; Italian: verita'; and French: vérité, which indicates that the truth is something that can be verified. In the language of science, truth is often represented by mathematical equations that can be balanced, replicated, and proven.

सत्य-Hindi pronounced saty (sat-tia)	真実–Japanese pronounced shinjitsu
Правда-Russian for truth-pravda	Αλήθεια-Greek word pronounced alítheia
真相Mandarin (Zhēnxiàng) (jin-si-yang)	진실 Korean (jinsil sounds like tin-shed)

The idea of truth is universal among all peoples and in all languages. Every ethnic group and nationality has a word meaning truth, with a

---

17 https://www.dictionary.com/browse/truth quoted on June 09, 2021.

common definition. And while U.S. Navy sailors are taught to cherish and seek the truth, there are people in this world who will always place self-interest and obtaining power as a higher aim. George Orwell, the author of *Animal Farm* and *1984*, warned that "The further a society drifts from the truth, the more it will hate those that speak it."[18]

Perhaps it is naïve to believe everyone is biologically and spiritually preset to seek and tell the truth, but I firmly do. If you have ever been polygraphed for a U.S. Government security clearance, you have experienced direct evidence of this hypothesis. Think about how you felt when someone you trusted lied to you. This too is further evidence of our natural longing for truth. Our minds, souls, and hearts want the truth. We all want to know why we are here and what the meaning of life is. We are all fascinated by the intricacies and complexity of the natural world, such as the earth, the eye, the nucleus of an atom, and the beauty of an exploding firework. While in command of USS THE SULLIVANS (DDG-68), and throughout my Navy career, I believed it was my job to harness and enhance the curious nature of sailors by example. I asked lots of questions and always tried my best to pursue knowledge and the truth passionately, thinking that if I did, others will follow.

Critical thinking and pursuit of truth require hard work and discipline. One must be detached from ego, and not be vested in any particular answer or course of action. The truth should be above self-interest and personal gain. Human nature and selfish desire make this endeavor difficult and cloud our search for truth. But as Albert Einstein said, "the important thing is not to stop questioning."[19] Critical thinking starts with

---

18 https://www.goodreads.com/quotes/8204871-the-further-a-society-drifts-from-the-truth-the-more taken June 09, 2021.

19 https://www.pbs.org/wgbh/nova/einstein/wisd-nf.html Nova Einstein quotes, June 9, 2021.

asking good questions and then sifting through all the possible answers. Cherry-picking data and bending it to fit a predetermined theory or hypothesis is not good science nor part of critical thinking. When a person's financial interests are tied to a position, project, or program, the truth becomes muddled and hard to discern. The U.S. Navy and USS THE SULLIVANS (DDG-68) demanded an unbiased, detached pursuit of knowledge and truth. So that is what I tried to do and pushed sailors to do the same. It was not always fun, but in the end, it was rewarding and the right course of action.

Spiral galaxy (Pinwheel Galaxy M101) and
NOAA satellite photo of Hurricane Andrew 1992

Whether one's passion is spiral galaxies or hurricanes, inspiring cross-disciplinary critical thinking at sea and ashore leads to discovery and the formulation of new ideas, which drive innovation. Many captains use egalitarian war councils or advisory groups at sea to cut through the rank structure and improve a ship's tactical prowess. Participants in these groups are usually selected for their critical thinking skills and passion for perfection. Knowledge, not rank or time in service, is the currency of such groups. For example, in USS THE SULLIVANS (DDG-68), our war council consisted of the most knowledgeable watch standers and technicians we had amongst us. Our smartest and most knowledgeable Aegis Combat System expert was an FC2 (firecontrolman second class) we called Rain Man. He had memorized Aegis schematics and knew all the facts and figures of the system like no one else. We relied on his knowledge often to improve pre-planned responses, hone tactics, and prep for exercise missile shoots. THE SULLIVANS war council consisted of all different rates and skills. Everyone had an equal voice and seat at the table. The goal was always the pursuit of truth and the best way to achieve the desired combat outcome.

When our sailors worked together across different rates and commands in pursuit of the truth amazing things happened. This is the essence of teamwork and is rooted in the Golden Rule: do unto others as you would have them do unto you. This simple recipe for success requires hard work and constant focus by all hands, especially those in leadership roles. Hypocrisy and insincerity can quickly destroy all the good that come from critical thinking and pursuit of the truth. U.S. Navy sailors are especially gifted at detecting hypocrisy and falsehood. This often helps those in leadership roles do the right thing, because sailors are always watching, listening, and taking note of how their leaders act and what they say. When there is a mismatch, they are not shy about speaking truth to power, as that is how they have been trained.

The U.S. Navy's emphasis on critical thinking and pursuit of the truth is central to the rise and maintenance of history's most powerful fleet. U.S. Navy sailors use, maintain, and improve upon the most advanced radars, sonars, and weapon systems in the world. Critical thinking is required to keep the fleet running and ready to fight tonight as per the CNO's direction. U.S. Navy sailors come from all walks of life and represent the nation well in terms of diversity, intelligence, and work ethic. Critical-thinking skills are developed throughout their service, and these skills are highly sought after by U.S. and international companies when our sailors retire or leave the Navy.

Perhaps someday a former USS THE SULLIVANS (DDG-68) sailor will put forth a new theory about the galactic Coriolis effect, the multi-verse, or the curvature of space-time. Maybe a new link between the shape of the earth, the eye, the nucleus of an atom, and how a fire work explodes will be found? The truth is out there and it is our mission to go find it. In USS THE SULLIVANS (DDG-68), everyone in the crew was taught, trained, and encouraged to pursue the truth and flex their critical-thinking skills. The shared belief in the overarching importance of the pursuit of the truth made us better professional mariners and warfighters and kept USS THE SULLIVANS (DDG-68) on the path to excellence.

CHAPTER 8

BOOMERS, MILLENNIALS, GENERATION Z, & SSOPP

2017 Pacific Grove High School graduation ceremony Pacific Grove, CA

"Millennials (aka Generation Y) are great at social media (Facebook, Google+, LinkedIn, Twitter, Tumblr, Instagram, Flickr, Snapchat,

Pinterest, YouTube, Vimeo, and Periscope) but lack time tested social skills (patience, humility, active listening, respect for parents, teachers, elderly)" Ramesh Lohia[20]

When I took command of USS THE SULLIVANS (DDG-68) in June 2006, I was 39 years old and probably considered old and a boomer by those in their late teens and twenties. Technically I am part of Generation X, but my attitude and character would probably trigger many young people today. I was, and am, a product of my environment, education, and work experience. My family and friends and spiritual beliefs also greatly impact the way I think, act, and communicate. A strict Roman Catholic upbringing, military college, and the U.S. Navy set my moral compass and pointed me towards a path of learning, self-confidence, and what I consider a pure pursuit of the truth.

But my sailors and my own children constantly reminded me that my ideas of truth, history, and pop culture were woefully out of touch. To them my way of thinking was stereotypical of the boomer generation and the reason for all of the world's problems. My predilection for making references and analogies to the TV sitcoms of my youth, such as *Leave it to Beaver* and *Three's Company*, did not help my case, and my pop references always seemed to miss the mark with twenty somethings on a steady diet of social media platforms I knew nothing about. For many millennials/Generation Z young adults I came across as an out of touch, Mr. Magoo—yet another reference from my youth that they would not understand. I realized I needed to bridge this gap to communicate more effectively with the crew. Luckily for me the U.S. Navy provided a shared set of values that we could all relate to.

---

20 https://www.goodreads.com/author/show/16987159.Ramesh_Lohia. This quote was taken from author Romesh Lohia circa 2019.

The U.S. Navy officially began October 13, 1775, when the Second Continental Congress passed a resolution which created the Continental Navy. Since that time until today, the U.S. Navy has been manned by young people, the vast majority of whom are between 20 and 30 years old. John Paul Jones was only 32 when he commanded the USS BONHOMME RICHARD at the Battle of Flamborough Head, in 1779. The Sullivan brothers were all in their twenties (20-27) when they died at the Naval Battle of Guadalcanal in 1942. John Paul Jones and the Sullivan brothers were the millennials or Generation Z of their eras. The U.S. Navy runs on young American blood and always has. In order to work efficiently and win wars at sea, U.S. Navy captains have to communicate and motivate young people. This has been done well over the centuries by maintaining formalized shared values. These specially tuned shared values enabled young men and women of each successive American generation to learn, train, and fight effectively at sea.

In the modern U.S. Navy, these shared sea-going values have evolved into the Sound Shipboard Operating Principles and Procedures (SSOPP). SSOPP is a process-improvement philosophy trained, preached, and exclusively practiced by the U.S. Navy. It is not unlike some business process-improvement programs such as Total Quality Management and Lean Six Sigma, but specifically evolved and made for sailors and the tasks they perform at sea. SSOPP is rooted in critical thinking and drives sailors to continuously learn and improve their level of knowledge, performance, and teamwork. All sailors, new recruits to senior admirals, must learn, live, and practice these principles and procedures at sea and ashore. The bottom line up front is SSOPP is proven and works. It is what keeps nuclear-powered aircraft carriers and ballistic missile submarines crewed by millennials and Generation Z operating smoothly and ready for battle.

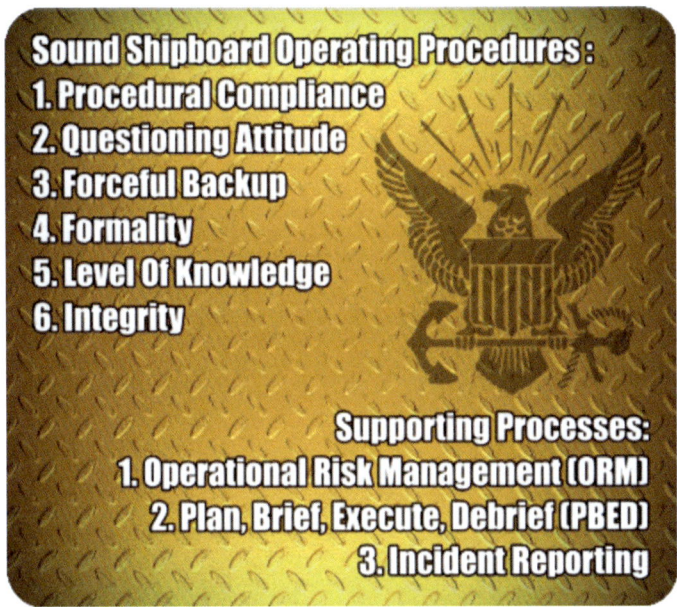

From SSOPP CNSFINST 3500.5 series watchstander's guide

Flight deck operations CVN-77 in Mediterranean Sea 2015

Today's U.S. Navy consists of over 325,000 active duty personnel, 75 % of whom are in the millennial/Generation Z age range (i.e., born in the 1980s to 2000s). U.S. Navy sailors are taught, trained, drilled, and tested on SSOPP. There are six core principles (labelled as procedures in the graphic above) and three supporting processes which empower today's sailors to safely operate the world's most technologically advanced warships, submarines, and aircraft in high-stress environments and succeed. So why aren't we teaching these same principles to all American middle and high school-age kids? Think of the benefits to the nation if America's teenagers learned how to operate in high-stress, extremely competitive environments and succeed.

In USS THE SULLIVANS (DDG-68) in June 2006 and up to the present, SSOPP was and is taught, preached, and practiced every day. I can attest that it helped bridge my generation gap with sailors. SSOPP and its supporting processes are part of every brief, evolution, task, and mission in the U.S. Navy. SSOPP is like a computer programming language for young brains. Once it takes root, it enhances the way sailors interact with their environment and shipmates. It is the essence of teamwork and essential to everything that happens on U.S. Navy platforms on, below, or above the sea. Ships and sailors that take SSOPP to heart tend to succeed, while those who do not are soon left behind. It helped me greatly during my command tour, and continues to be something I preach and teach today.

What are SSOPP?

The Navy's SSOPP (Sound Shipboard Operating Principles and Procedures) are simple to understand.[21] SSOPP formally entered the Navy around 2004 but are not rooted in any particular generation or history. They are proven concepts in peace-time and war that everyone can understand and use. SSOPP formulate the basis of Navy operational culture and stimulate critical thinking and continual organizational improvement over time when followed.

1. **Procedural Compliance:** Following written guidance and procedures carefully. Read the instructions before completing a task. Use the official references, technical manuals, and guidance. In the U.S. Navy there is a written procedure, checklist, or maintenance requirement for everything. Most of these were written in blood, meaning they were written down or updated following a mishap where someone was hurt or killed because the previous procedure was incorrect or could not be properly followed. Procedural compliance is nothing more than following instructions as if your life depended on it.

2. **Questioning Attitude:** According to the Navy, questioning attitude is both a critical thinking skill and an exercise in vigilance. It requires a sailor to think and stay focused on the task at hand. When a step, process, or procedure does not make sense it is okay to question it and seek additional information or guidance. In other words, one needs to care about what they are doing and remain mindful of the purpose and the desired outcome, and not just blindly follow a checklist or procedure. When a sailor hears the phrase, "but we have always done it

---

21 This summation on SSOPP is based on material in COMNAVSURFORINST 3500.5 dated February 19, 2015.

this way ...," it should trigger them to engage their questioning attitude and ensure they are following the correct procedure for the task at hand. Think before you do.

3. **Forceful Backup:** Sailors are required to think for themselves and help their shipmates ensure unclear orders and tasks are questioned and clarified. In short, one should be their brothers' keeper and back their shipmates up, especially when performing dangerous duties or tasks. The saying "If you see something, say something" is a civilian form of the U.S. Navy's concept of forceful backup. Keep your eyes and ears open and lookout for your shipmates at all times.

4. **Formality**: Formality is the rigorous adherence to established rules, customs, or norms. Formality drives focus and attention to detail. Following formal protocols and customs keeps sailors on task and prevents them from being complacent and making mistakes. Examples of formality include standard commands, verbatim repeat backs, wearing dress uniforms properly, and detailed watch turnovers. Formality means being professional.

5. **Level of Knowledge**: Sailors must understand the concepts, facts, and science behind everything they do so that they have the requisite knowledge before they can safely perform a task, follow a procedure, or execute complex orders. Sailors are required to achieve a minimum, formal personal qualification standard (PQS) before being qualified for any watch, significant position, or supervisory role. In the Navy, level of knowledge can be demonstrated in many ways: written exams, oral boards, or performing a task under supervision. Sailors are taught to be professionally curious and are rewarded for exceeding

minimum standards. Sailors are conditioned to continually improve their level of knowledge.

6. **Integrity:** Integrity is honesty and serves as the basis for all the SSOPP. When asked, most U.S. Navy sailors would respond that integrity is doing the right thing even when no one is looking. Sailors are taught in boot camp never to lie, cheat, or steal nor tolerate those who do. Integrity also means wholeness and trust. Sailors who lack integrity have short and unproductive careers in the U.S. Navy.

Silly image of what a fancy French pickle (PIQL) might look like

FFPIQL … Fancy French PIQL

The U.S. Navy uses many silly mnemonic devices to aid in training and memorization. A mnemonic is a pattern of letters or mental image that helps people remember a longer acronym or a series of items in a larger topic. The SSOPP can be quickly recalled by picturing a fancy French pickle, which provides a memorable mental image for the rearranged SSOPP bullet points under the acronym: F F P I Q L. **F**ormality, **F**orceful

Backup, **P**rocedural Compliance, **I**ntegrity, **Q**uestioning Attitude, and **L**evel of Knowledge. When a sailor is told to think of a fancy French pickle, it often results in a juvenile laugh or giggle as this image is absurd and somewhat phallic. Sailors cannot forget this image once they hear it, which brings forth the acronym FFPIQL causing SSOPP to be more easily remembered. Silly imagined mnemonic devices are a useful method to achieve rapid learning for sailors, so they are used and used again across generations.

In addition to the six, sound shipboard operating principles listed above, that is, Formality, Forceful Backup, Procedural Compliance, Integrity, Questioning Attitude, and Level of Knowledge, the Navy uses three processes across the fleet. They are operational risk management, planning-briefing-execution-debriefing (PBED), and incident reporting. These three supporting processes are similar to the management techniques private companies, government agencies, or public institutions utilize to effectively run their organizations. In the Navy, everyone is expected to embrace and use these processes in conjunction with the six sound shipboard operating principles described above.

The Navy's SSOPP are proven principles which have held up over time. Go visit any operational U.S. Navy warship, submarine, aircraft squadron, or SEAL team today and you can see these principles and procedures at work. SSOPP are simple to teach and even more effective when sailors believe they are following them for a cause greater than self. The teamwork, camaraderie, and sense of purpose that spring from SSOPP drive sailors–millennials/Generation Z-to see the importance of FFPIQL and, thus, sustain its belief and practice across the generations.

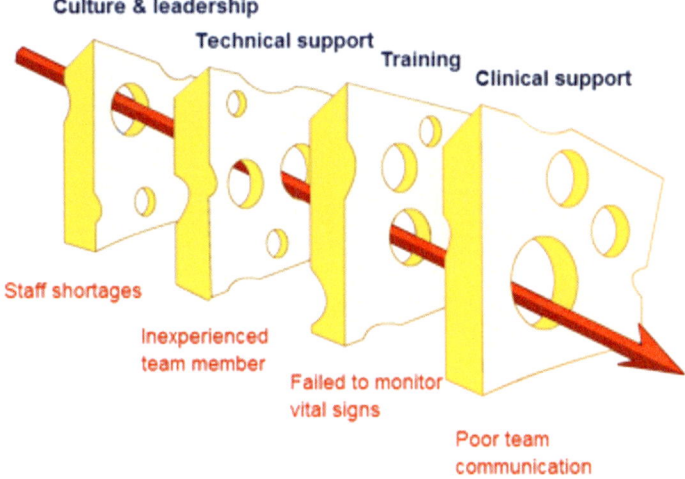

The Swiss cheese model of accident causation

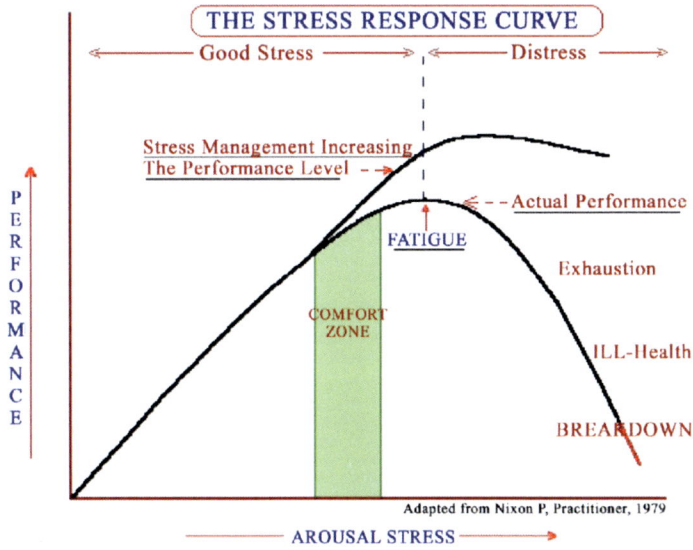

The stress response curve adapted from Nixon P. Practitioner, 1979

SSOPP evolved to reduce human error and improve performance at sea. SSOPP help close the holes in the Swiss cheese model of accident causation and keep sailors in the comfort/green zone along the stress response curve. Both the Swiss cheese model of accident causation and the stress response curve are referenced often by U.S. Navy training specialists and military instructors when teaching SSOPP. U.S. Navy training on SSOPP also relies heavily on case studies, which demonstrate how disaster struck crews and warships that forgot or ignored the six core principles and procedures of SSOPP–Formality, Forceful backup, Procedural compliance, Integrity, Questioning attitude, and Level of knowledge.

Generations and generations of U.S. Navy sailors have built upon the corporate knowledge learned from their predecessors, especially during war-time. SSOPP (aka FFPIQL) emerged from condensing more than two centuries of lessons learned. The simple mnemonic device FFPIQL empowers sailors to prevent accidents, stay alert, and work at sea safely. Leaders rely on SSOPP to accomplish complex missions in the most dangerous environments around the globe.

USS THE SULLIVANS (DDG-68) sailor busting rust

*USS THE SULLIVANS (DDG-68) subject matter expert
explaining M203 grenade launcher*

"We are what we repeatedly do. Excellence, then, is not an act, but a habit." Will Durant[22]

Whether a person enlists in the Navy or works at McDonalds or Microsoft, adopting the Navy's SSOPP would help both the individual and the team reduce human error, improve efficiency, and promote critical thinking. Using SSOPP boosts self-confidence and reduces anxiety. The battle tested Navy SSOPP allow young men and women from all walks of life to succeed as sailors; and has made the U.S. Navy the most dominant sea power in world history. Today the Navy and the nation entrust our way of life and national security to millennials and Generation Z who are following SSOPP.

The preceding paragraphs might sound like a cheesy boomer era info-mercial or even straight up propaganda, but, most assuredly they are not. SSOPP works and are constantly tested and re-tested in the real world of U.S. Navy operations at sea. SSOPP work best when leaders incorporate them directly into their standing orders and instructions, and then lead by example, practicing what they preach. SSOPP are fun-damental to successful and safe evolutions, missions, and operations at sea. SSOPP not only reduce human error and improve battle efficiency, but also strengthen character by forcing sailors to think for themselves.

Prior to the adoption of SSOPP, U.S. Navy sailors followed similar princi-ples and procedures, albeit under different names and acronyms. Today FFPIQL and other silly mnemonics work well to capture over 230 years of hard-earned lessons and carry the SSOPP across the generation gap that naturally occurs at sea between older captains and young sailors.

22 https://www.brainyquote.com/quotes/will_durant_145967 downloaded July 08, 2021. Will Durant is a famous author and historian who put these words in English based on the philosophy of Socrates.

If the image of a fancy French pickle helps U.S. Navy sailors to develop strong character by following the principles of Formality, Forceful backup, Procedural compliance, Integrity, Questioning attitude, and Level of knowledge than *c'est la vie*. For as the ancient Greek philosopher, Heraclitus said, "A man's character is his fate."[23]

---

23 https://www.brainyquote.com/topics/character-quotes downloaded September 7, 2021.

CHAPTER 9

CHARACTER MAINTENANCE 101

Photo of President Lincoln 1863 by Mathew Brady

1553 French portrait of Lucius Quinctius Cincinnatus
published by Guillaume Rouille

Character maintenance is something most of us do not take the time to focus on every day, but we should. For U.S. Navy sailors, developing a strong positive character is vital for success at sea and ashore. Character is the force that aligns a sailor's moral compass. It guides them over the horizon and through the stormy seas of life's decisions by providing a voyage plan and clear track to follow. Dictionary.com defines character as "the aggregate of features and traits that form the individual nature of some person or thing."[24] I like to think of character as the vessel that contains my personality and soul. Character is also the accumulation of an individual's decisions and actions. Our character or, more specifically, our moral character evolves over the course of our lives, hopefully for the better.

Men of great character such as Abraham Lincoln and Lucius Quinctius Cincinnatus were guided by virtue and heralded for their example. They are role models today because they stood for something more than self, more than the pursuit of self-interest, power, and money. These great men realized that their character was their most precious possession. In the end all we truly have in this life is our character. It is what we will leave behind in people's hearts and minds, and take with us to the hereafter. Our character houses and drives our moral compass, and lets us know right from wrong.

U.S. Navy sailors are indoctrinated and trained to cherish the core values of honor, courage, and commitment from day one at bootcamp. If the U.S. Navy could it would inject these into each sailor's arm via a hypodermic needle, but core values do not work that way. They have to be learned and synchronized with each individual's character. Our character helps us discern right from wrong, good from evil, and kindness from

---

24 https://www.dictionary.com/browse/character downloaded June 14, 2021.

cruelty. The U.S. Navy wants sailors to become independent minded, professional warfighters but also to be thoughtful, polite, and just. This dichotomy can sometimes present sailors with a moral dilemma, especially if they are struggling to internalize the concepts of honor, courage, and commitment.

How do sailors know where the line between right and wrong is? Based on my observations over more than 33 years working with U.S. Navy sailors on active duty and as a civilian military contractor, I believe each individual's moral compass is initially set and calibrated by their parents, families, friends, and home environments. Everyone's moral compass needs realignment from time to time, but our initial idea of what is right and wrong does not come to us in boot camp, officer candidate school, or the U.S. Naval Academy. Our character is formed before we walk up the brow of a ship or open the door to the captain's cabin.

When I was in command of USS THE SULLIVANS (DDG-68), I would have every new sailor who reported aboard schedule a formal visit to my cabin for a meeting. When they arrived at my door we would then sit down and talk. After introductions and a brief discussion about expectations, duties, and the ship's schedule, I would ask them to show me where they were from. I kept a large U.S. atlas in my desk and would pull it out and have them circle or star the city or town they came from and ask them for their autograph. This sometimes caused some strange looks. I learned this practice from a former commanding officer and thought it a great icebreaker and way to learn about who these sailors were as individuals. I had to expand this practice and buy a world atlas as I discovered more and more of our sailors were not originally from the United States.

Getting sailors to open-up about their upbringing and life before the Navy provided a window into their character. It also helped me remember their names, hopes, and aspirations while making them understand they were an important part of our team. You can learn a lot about a person if you know where they are from and how they spent their formative years. I enjoyed these discussions and looked forward to each one. Over time my atlases grew full of signatures and stories. USS THE SULLIVANS (DDG-68) had a very diverse crew in 2006, with sailors from almost every state and territory in the union and many from overseas.

With such a diverse crew, and culture, society, and America changing so fast, a clear boundary between what was right and what was wrong was not as visible as I had thought. Several years back I participated in a seminar discussion with Mrs. Diana West, the author of a book entitled *"The Death of the Grown-Up."* Her thesis was that American culture has slipped into a permanent state of adolescence, and that danger is lurking as our collective political correctness has made us spineless. I disagreed with her premise, but as I listened carefully to her arguments and facts there did seem to be some cause for concern. For young sailors joining the fleet who were new to the concepts of honor, courage, and commitment and SSOPP, perhaps clarification was required about what was right and wrong in a U.S. Navy warship. The "thou shall not" list seemed clear to me but might not have been for someone just out of boot camp with a misaligned moral compass:

- No drinking on ships underway or inport unless authorized for special events.
- No illegal drug taking onboard or ashore: zero tolerance is the Navy policy.
- No sex or fraternization onboard.

- No sleeping on watch.
- No fistfights onboard.
- No sexual harassment.
- No selling stuff to junior sailors (i.e., using rank to make money from subordinates).
- No surfing internet porn on Navy computers.
- No giving away secrets or blogging about operations.
- No bullying, hazing, or disrespecting shipmates.
- No racism or racist language.

I thought this prohibitive list was common sense, but as my character was formed, shaped, and molded by my strict Roman Catholic, Baby Boomer/Generation X upbringing, what I thought was obvious needed to be clearly stated. I realized after many meetings with newly reported sailors that they were not me. They did not grow up where I did. They were not shaped by the same environment, religion, and education that I had. They were different and that was okay.

Although her thesis did not resonate with me, I do recall Mrs. Diana West stating that the military was one of the last bastions of virtue in American culture. Hearing her say that made me feel proud to be part of the military. I believe most people that serve in the Navy feel the same way regardless of their rank, age, or branded generation. I got this same feeling when I talked with our sailors. I also learned that sailors cannot know the captain's expectations until they are clearly explained. While this seems like common sense, there are many leaders who do not take the time to explain what is expected. I too had been guilty of this as a department head and division officer.

Being a commanding officer is like being a parent in many ways. Your crew is your family at sea, and your actions and words have meaning and serve as a model, good or bad, for your sailors and your children. Leadership is not about keeping people happy but treating them fairly, giving them hope, and guiding them down the right path to contribute to our Navy and nation. Today's young adults I would argue are smarter in many ways than those of us who grew up before the internet. Like our generation, today's young sailors are volunteers but from a different, perhaps slightly more self-indulgent and confused, chapter in America's history. The overwhelming majority of Sailors that signed my atlases were men and women of good character, who volunteered to serve and wanted to succeed just as much as I did.

Today the United States does not have a Cold War to fight with tanks and troops ready to drive into the Fulda Gap but whose enemies lurk in the shadows—mysterious, cowardly bearded men who think their religion is better than ours. They have established a beachhead in far-away ungovernable lands, hide in caves, post propaganda on the internet, and send the poor and misinformed to do their dirty work. There are cyber-hackers and criminal drug cartels who lie, cheat, and steal for money and power. Some say climate change, racism, and economic inequality are the biggest threats to the United States while others point to China, Russia, Iran, and North Korea. The post-Cold War, post-9/11 world is turbulent, dynamic, and moving fast in an unknown direction. Today's uncertainty and growing instability require all of us to maintain and strengthen both our character and resolve.

Sitting in the captain's chair in USS THE SULLIVANS (DDG-68), I realized that my sense of right and wrong was based on a belief system that was unique to my upbringing and environment, but that felt universal. When I was young, homosexuality, abortion, pre-marital sex, and lots of other things were considered wrong and even illegal—but now they are not. If you were raised in a strict old-world Roman Catholic family that developed its values and moral judgements pre-Vatican II, how do you convey your ideals to a sailor who comes from a secular single-parent family and is fed a steady diet of rap music and social media? Could that sailor empathize and imagine in their mind how you see the world? Probably not unless there were some shared values and beliefs that could be sorted out. And the only way I found to do this effectively was through consistent discussion and dialogue: not email—not mission statements—but old-fashioned talking.

Sailors have to understand before they can successfully execute orders and tasks, and captains have to trust if we want them to lead. This can be done, and I think that is the ultimate gratification of leading, coaching, and teaching. Finding the right words, analogies, or parable that resonated with sailors brought me much satisfaction. When they understood my expectations and point of view, they could exceed my minimum standards.

Over my Navy career I have greatly enjoyed having discussions about right and wrong with sailors. I appreciated their views, especially when their upbringing and generation were distinct from my own. I learned something new in almost every interaction. Frank discussions about Navy standards and values are always interesting conversations and happen all the time in every space on every ship. The bottom line is the person in charge of any group of people needs to understand where the line between right and wrong is, articulate it clearly to the crew, and always stay on the right side of that line. The line between right and wrong cannot be ambiguous or cloudy. From the smoke break to the captain's cabin and everywhere in between, sailors want to know where the line between right and wrong is and expect their leaders to set the example through their personal behavior and professional integrity. While the Navy's cultural boundaries may shift from time to time, good leaders do not let their character and integrity slip. Character maintenance is a daily requirement.

CHAPTER 10

GET OVER YOURSELF —
IT AIN'T ABOUT YOU — MISSION FIRST

VOYAGE STATISTICS
26, 250 NM STEAMED
2,842,363 gal DFM burned
2,226,561 gal of Potable H20 used
37,114 rounds of ammo shot
4 X Turkish Straits, 2 X STROG, 2 X Straits of Messina

USS THE SULLIVANS (DDG-68) deployment statistics 2006-2007

In the U.S. Navy, sailors are trained and conditioned to complete the mission. The catch phrase one hears over and over is "mission first, people always." This means that while both mission and people are essential, the primary goal is to complete the mission. It is a leader's duty to always take care of his or her people, but mission accomplishment is paramount. Selflessness is required because it should never be about you. Sailors can tell when sincerity and selflessness are lacking. Ego and pride have their place and can drive captains to success, but in the end it is not about you, your ego, or your personal desires. Captains and commanders are expendable and replaceable. There are always dozens of U.S. Navy captains and commanders waiting in the wings for their chance to sit in the captain's chair.

Command at sea demands striking the right balance between mission accomplishment, taking care of sailors, and managing one's ego. This is what was going through my mind in the fall of 2006 as our ship was preparing for an independent six-month deployment to the Mediterranean and Black Seas. I also needed to learn and understand our new mission, figure out how to best accomplish it, and get the crew to do their best to make it work.

On November 27, 2006, USS THE SULLIVANS (DDG-68) departed Mayport for its fourth six-month deployment since the ship was commissioned into service nine years earlier on April 19, 1997. Families gathered on the pier to watch the ship cast off its lines. For those that have seen and done this before, it is a very sad day for those left standing on the pier. My own family watched as we pulled away and then headed to Mayport beach to wave at the ship as it left the jetties of St. John's River. I remember seeing my wife and kids waving from the jetties. They looked so happy and were smiling but were probably already sad inside. I was too busy to realize this at that moment. The ship's scheduled training and first day at sea drew my attention away from my own thoughts and family. It would hit me half way across the Atlantic. I would miss them all very much. Email, occasional packages, and rare phone calls would be how our crew would communicate with loved ones for the next six months. It was better than nothing but just barely, especially when those we loved were sad, lonely, and longed for a bear hug from their deployed sailors.

USS THE SULLIVANS (DDG-68) was to transit across the Atlantic Ocean with USS KAUFFMAN (FFG-59), an Oliver Hazard Perry-class frigate based in Norfolk. We were to meet up with KAUFFMAN in a couple of days, then both ships were to deploy in support of the Global War on Terrorism (GWOT) and U.S. Commander Sixth Fleet's theater-specific mission requirements. KAUFFMAN and THE SULLIVANS would in chop to (i.e., come under the control of) U.S. Sixth Fleet based in Naples and then go our separate ways. KAUFFMAN would sail to the Gulf of Guinea and North Africa, and THE SULLIVANS would head south and east across the Mediterranean, and later into the Black Sea.

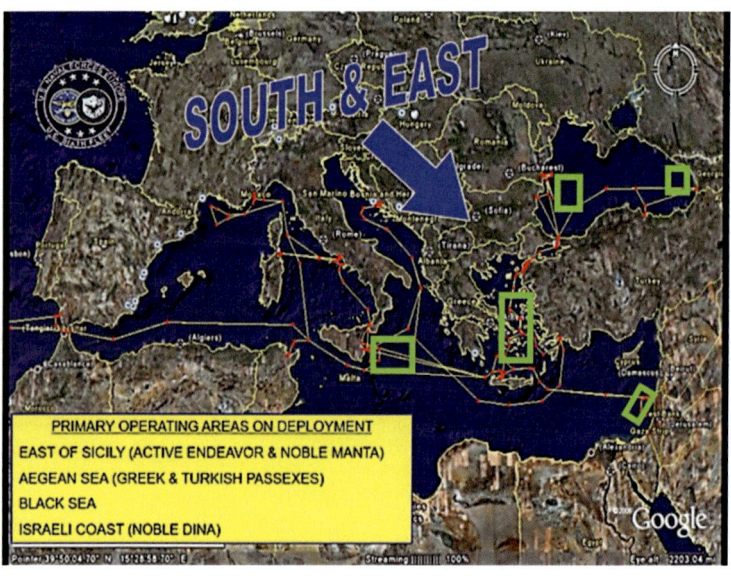

USS THE SULLIVANS (DDG-68) Operating Area 2006-2007

NATO Active Endeavour patch

Sixth Fleet's mission meshed nicely with the Chief of Naval Operations' (CNO) concept of a 1,000-ship Navy, which meant bringing allied navies into a unified partnership with the U.S. fleet to fight the GWOT. NATO countries in the Mediterranean Sea were conducting Operation Active Endeavour (OAE). OAE began soon after the 9/11 terrorist attacks to deter, defend, disrupt and protect against terrorist activity in and around the Mediterranean Sea. It was an official NATO Article 5 operation, marking the first time ever that NATO nations and navies had initiated an official collective defence operation. According to NATO's website, Article 5 specified that:

"The Parties agree that an armed attack against one or more of them in Europe or North America shall be considered an attack against them all and consequently they agree that, if such an armed attack occurs, each of them, in exercise of the right of individual or collective self-defence recognized by Article 51 of the Charter of the United Nations, will assist the Party or Parties so attacked by taking forthwith, individually and in concert with the other Parties, such action as it deems necessary, including the use of armed force, to restore and maintain the security of the North Atlantic area."[25]

NATO's Article 5 was the linchpin of the NATO alliance. It was also designed to counter and prevent an attack against a specific enemy: the Soviet Union. Throughout the entirety of the Cold War, NATO's Article 5 collective defense clause had never been activated. Following the 9/11 attacks, however, NATO nations decided that Al-Qaeda's attack on the U.S. required a collective response by the entirety of NATO. This was a major turning point and milestone for NATO and marked the dawn of a new era, the post-Cold War, post 9/11 world.

---

25 https://www.nato.int/cps/en/natohq/topics_110496.htm#:~:text=Article%205%20 provides%20that%20if,to%20assist%20the%20Ally%20attacked, downloaded June 17, 2021.

Commander, Task Force 67 meeting with Romanians in 2007

French Navy Rafale fighter working with DDG-68 in 2007 in support of OAE

A vital part of USS THE SULLIVANS (DDG-68) mission during this deployment was to help new NATO and non-NATO navies participate in OAE.[26] Additionally, THE SULLIVANS was tasked with building maritime domain awareness, theater security cooperation, and maritime safety and security for the Mediterranean and Black Sea areas of responsibilty. These vital diplomatic and security tasks would translate into face-to-face training and engagement opportunities between THE SULLIVANS crew members and young men and women of partnership navies and nations around the Mediterranean and Black Seas. Our mission this time around was not about breaking things and killing people, but building lasting friendships and synchronizing training with nascent NATO and non NATO nations such as Croatia, Romania, Bulgaria, Georgia, and Israel.

Getting a multi-mission U.S. Navy destroyer ready for a six-month deployment requires Herculean effort by the crew. There are dozens of basic phase certifications, engineering inspections, logistical preparations and at-sea training events which require 12 to 18 months of time and millions of dollars in maintenance and training costs. The focus of all this effort is to be ready to fight on, above, and below the sea anywhere in the world our political leaders decide to send us. And while USS THE SULLIVANS (DDG-68) was certainly ready to fight any enemy that might come our way, we now also had to be able to engage with diplomacy and grace, embark U.S. ambassadors and foreign dignitaries, and put on soirees suitable for the rich and famous of Europe, North Africa, and Asia Minor. Our mission was not what we had expected during our work-up phase, but we would accomplish it with passion and professionalism to the best of our ability. Missiles, torpedoes, five-inch shells, and machine

---

26 https://shape.nato.int/missionarchive/operation-active-endeavour downloaded June 15, 2021.

guns would take a backseat to rock music, ship sports teams, ice sculptures, and catered events on the flight deck.

USS THE SULLIVANS (DDG-68) rock band Keelhauled practicing in Sonar 4

Keelhauled practicing on flight deck Split, Croatia January 2007

Our secret weapon and main battery on this deployment was not in a vertical launch tube but kept deep below the main deck in Sonar 4. This was the only compartment on the ship with enough space, electrical power, and air-conditioning to support this small elite group of warriors: USS THE SULLIVANS' own American rock and roll band. The band was made up of junior enlisted sailors and chief petty officers. The drummer was a firecontrolman second class (FC2) and the lead singer was an electronics technician third class (ET3). We had a very talented sonar technician third class (STG3) on lead guitar and two chief petty officers who played base and rhythm guitar while providing the adult supervision … sometimes.

The band named themselves Keelhauled, after the old seagoing form of punishment and potential execution where a miscreant sailor would be tied to a line, thrown overboard, and then dragged beneath the ship bow to stern or athwartships across the keel. Barnacles and marine growth on the ship's hull would shred tissue and cause immense pain if the victim was not fortunate enough to drown first.[27] Keelhauled was a great name for our rock and roll band, and the crew especially liked it. It symbolized how tough Navy life could be, but also satirically signaled to make the best of the situation and have a little fun along the way.

Keelhauled was not a polished and scripted act but more of an old-fashioned American garage band. They covered songs they liked and even wrote some of their own. Their sound was unique, slow-roasted southern-dipped metal blended with a little bit of country and a hint of glam rock pop. Keelhauled was as good as any bar band in Jacksonville,

---

27 https://en.wikipedia.org/wiki/Keelhauling. From the Dutch word "Kielhalen," to drag beneath the keel. Downloaded June 17, 2021.

Florida, or any American city. They enjoyed their time on stage and rep-resented the United States and THE SULLIVANS very well.

In time the band's set list included songs by Lynyrd Skynyrd, Three Doors Down, Kiss, Jimmy Buffet, the Animals, Pearl Jam, and just about anything we asked them to learn. Our lead singer was deeply religious and would not sing any songs with profanity or explicit lyrics. This too worked to our benefit, and also led to other band members writing and singing their own tunes from time to time. Keelhauled was a hit every-where we went. And like any team that practices and plays together over and over, they got really good at what they did. Their music and vocals were smooth, clean, and loud. They had character and could adapt their style to suit any audience like the Blues Brothers—Dan Aykroyd and John Belushi—when they played at Bob's Country Bunker, chicken wire, smashed beer bottles and all. Their showmanship was top notch. Keelhauled was a band you would wait in line and pay a $10.00 cover to see on a Saturday night in Jacksonville.

Keelhauled live at Doors Club Constanta, Romania February 13, 2007

121

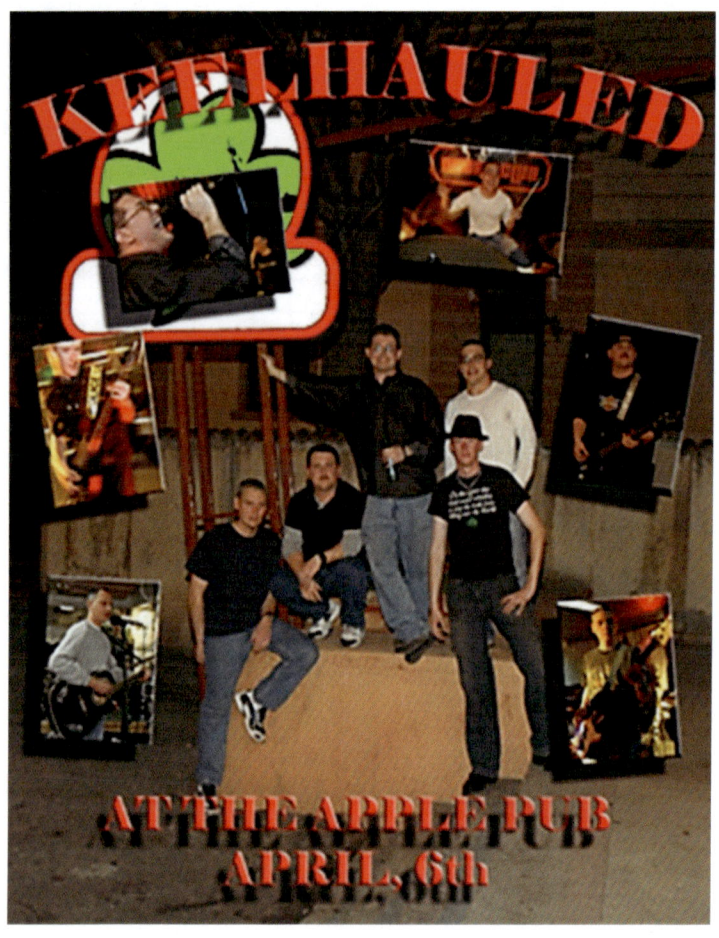

Keelhauled music poster from performance in Catania, Sicily April 6, 2007

Their performances began on the flight and mess decks but soon spread throughout Europe, North Africa, and Asia Minor. Keelhauled was a hit with the crew, foreign sailors, and dignitaries alike. They played on piers, street corners, clubs, and any venue we asked them to, always figuring out how to convert local electrical power available, and set up equipment for an extremely professional show. They did all this on their off-duty time and sacrificed their own liberty to entertain our crew and guests. Other crew members, including me, helped out as their roadies, security detail, and logisticians.

I served as their captain and also as the band manager, and worked hard to get them venues where they could be seen and showcase our *We Stick Together* spirit. Every time USS THE SULLIVANS entered a port in the Sixth Fleet area of responsibility (AOR), I would make formal calls on local military and civilian officials. These scripted meetings with local base commanders, government officials, and city mayors involved an exchange of pleasantries and minor diplomacy, and then the conversation would end with said officials asking me if there was anything they could do for the ship. As the nature of our mission developed, I realized this was a perfect opportunity to ask for an appropriate venue to showcase our band. When I explained that our ship had a rock and roll band and just wanted a place to play their music, most of the hosts jumped at the opportunity. Keelhauled worked cheap and took no money or gifts for their performances. They were playing for fun, their shipmates, and their nation, and that was payment enough.

Promotion poster Doors Club in English and Romanian

*Photo montage of Keelhauled performing live at the
Doors Club February 13, 2007 in Constanta*

One particularly memorable show occured during a port visit to Constanta, Romania. Constanta is a gritty industrial city on the Black Sea. In ancient times, Roman emperors would banish their enemies to this desolate eastern frontier town of the empire. Such was the fate of the famous Latin poet Ovid in 8 AD. Today Constanta is known for its multiculturalism, industry, and history as the ancient Roman port of Tomis. In Constanta, Keelhauled was allowed to headline at a nightclub/disco called the Doors Club. It was probably the nicest club in Constanta at the time, and Keelhauled would be the lead act on a Tuesday night. City officials, along with local Romanian military leaders, planned on attending.

The Doors Club was an American-themed venue that served burgers and beer. The club had seating for a few hundred patrons and a raised wooden stage with colored spot lights, perfect for rock and roll acts. All the booths and tables had a good view of the stage, and the acoustics and sound quality throughout the club were excellent. On this night the room was already crowded and packed with USS THE SULLIVANS sailors, Romanian military officials, local politicians, and probably a few Soviet-era spies. I was somewhat nervous and excited as I took a seat near the stage with some of our local Romanian military and civilian hosts. I was not sure how the band, our crew, and our American spirit would be received in what used to be the heart of the Warsaw Pact. Romania had only joined NATO in 2004, and their military had not operated much with the U.S. Navy at that point in time. The Romanian military and civilian leaders I was sitting with had been our enemies for decades, and now it was our mission to help them train and fight like us. This concert and get-together was our first real opportunity to befriend our new allies and show them who we really were.

The music began to play. Our lead singer took a sip of Sprite and then began singing "Simple Man" by Lynyrd Skynyrd. This three-chord ballad is classic Southern Fried Rock and was especially popular in THE SULLIVANS' home base of Jacksonville. The lyrics speak to humility and how one should live their life, "be a simple kind of man … be something you love and understand …" The words had deep meaning for our lead singer, our band, and our entire crew. It spoke to us and about us. It reflected where we came from and what we all truly wanted to be. Words have meaning, and when sung with passion they can even resonate in ears and minds not accustomed to the English language. Almost 6,000 miles from home in the Black Sea, USS THE SULLIVANS was on mission and on target.

Keelhauled sounded great and our crew began cheering, singing along, and dancing. I watched as our Romanian hosts smiled and loosened up. The club owner was extremely happy and locals started pouring in to see and hear all the excitement. By the end of the night everyone was on their feet, singing and shouting. At the end of the show, out of the blue, our lead guitarist got the urge to play the national anthem, but not the Jimmy Hendrix version, just a clean single-note version on the electric guitar. The crowd got very quiet as he started, but then to everyone's amazement, we all started singing the "Star Spangled Banner" at the top of our lungs. The night's libation and liquid merriment made us all a little braver, and for about a minute we were all rock stars, but above all patriots. The entire bar and all THE SULLIVANS crew sang our national anthem loud and proud, the Romanians right along side us. It was a true and spontaneous out-pouring of American spirit, and our new friends could see and feel it too.

DDG-68 command master chief (CMC) embarked in Romanian F-221

Romanian Sailor conducting VBSS training on DDG-68 with AK-74

Our fun in Constanta was followed by hard work ashore and at sea. We worked with the Romanian Navy and conducted visit, board, search, and seizure (VBSS) training. We trained at their facilities and they practiced on our ship, using Soviet-era weapons and tactics. They were exceptionally good at boarding and small squad tactics, and would have proven to be formidable enemies had the Cold War not ended. Where they needed help was with logistics, specifically NATO style helicopter operations at sea. Our flight deck team and subject matter experts worked alongside their crews and provided them with the level of knowledge and forceful backup they needed to get better. It was a very satisfying and productive exchange.

Keelhauled's music had fittingly opened the door to friendship at the Doors Club. The crew of USS THE SULLIVANS (DDG-68) had won over our new Romanian allies not by a show of force but with music, good old-fashioned American rock and roll music. Keelhauled's concert broke the ice and demonstrated our intent and national interest. Our billion-dollar high-tech warship had come in peace and friendship. USS THE SULLIVANS (DDG-68) was in the Black Sea to make friends and showcase our *We Stick Together* spirit. Constanta was shown a glimpse of the real America by real Americans, who demonstrated honor, courage, and commitment but also knew how to have fun. George, Francis, Joseph, Madison, and Albert would have been proud of their shipmates in USS THE SULLIVANS (DDG-68), who entered the Black Sea with guitars blazing and won the battle for friendship with our new Romanian allies. Music, not munitions, was the key to this victory.

CHAPTER 11

BEING MRS KRAVITZ IN THE BLACK SEA

CIA World Fact Book Map of Turkey and the Black Sea circa 2006

Mrs. Gladys Kravitz was Darrin and Samantha Stephen's nosy neighbor in the 1960s sitcom *Bewitched*. I grew up watching this TV show starring Elizabeth Montgomery and remember it transitioning from black and white to technicolor, which was amazing in and of itself. In the show, Samantha was a witch who was married to a mortal named Darrin. By simply wiggling her nose or snapping her fingers, Samantha could whip up a gourmet meal and do a week's worth of laundry in a microsecond. Real housewives and kids who had to do chores were jealous and day dreamed of having Samantha's ability for just a few hours. Samantha also had a dysfunctional, enmeshed witch family that caused chaos and hijinks every week. I watched every episode of that show, my favorites being a short sequence of episodes filmed on location in Salem and Gloucester entitled, "Samantha's Hot Bed Warmer," "Darrin on a Pedestal," and "Samantha's Bad Day in Salem."

Mrs. Kravitz was my least favorite character and made me cringe every time she popped into a scene. I genuinely did not like her annoying nosy habit of peering through windows and trying to catch the Stephens family doing something she deemed illegal, immoral, or criminal in the privacy of their own home. This feeling stuck with me decades later. Mrs. Gladys Kravitz represented the stereotypical nosy neighbor who was always spying on the house next door. She believed something was fishy but could never capture proof or get anyone to believe her. She was not likeable, but everyone could relate because every neighborhood had a Gladys Kravitz.[28]

In April 2007, while on deployment to the Sixth Fleet area of responsibility, USS THE SULLIVANS (DDG-68) was tasked to pass through the Bosporus and Dardanelles Straits a second time and head back into the Black Sea. Our mission was to continue training with the Bulgarian, Romanian, Turkish, and Georgian maritime forces. Political tensions in the Black Sea region were running high. USS THE SULLIVANS (DDG-68) was also in the area to conduct freedom of navigation operations and

---

28 The TV show I Dream of Jeannie, starring Barbara Eden, had a similar motif with Dr. Bellows, an Air Force colonel serving as a "Gladys Kravitz."

fulfill the obligations of the 1936 Montreux Convention with Turkey. The Montreux Convention regulated and limited the transit of naval warships into and out of the Black Sea. Sixth Fleet managed these transits carefully and followed the letter of the law so that the United States Government did not violate the treaty.

The Russians, however, did not want us there. They viewed the Black Sea as their millpond and on ramp to the Mediterranean and beyond. Geography and history drove their strategic thinking and military behavior. Despite the end of the Cold War there were still deep vestigial pockets of mistrust in Moscow, and the Russian Navy's hard-to-break habits formed from decades of anti-American practices. Officials in the Kremlin viewed USS THE SULLIVANS (DDG-68) as a direct challenge to their strategic maritime interests. Russian propaganda painted us as an armed and dangerous Gladys Kravitz, whose presence and influence was not wanted in the area, especially in and around Sevastopol and Crimea. We were trespassing and stirring things up with their neighbors.

This was not our mission nor our intention, but in the post-Cold War, Post-9/11 world, it is how our potential foe perceived us. The Russians were very displeased with the expansion of NATO, especially in the Black Sea. USS THE SULLIVANS (DDG-68) was sailing into hostile waters. Everyone in the crew had to comprehend the geopolitical context of our mission. Like our liberty briefs, we all had to know which neighborhoods to avoid, where the off limits areas were, and which actions would get us into trouble. There would be no soirees, ice sculptures, and martinis this time around. The Russians were not interested in Keelhauled and our musical abilities: they were focused on the kinetic potential of our Aegis warship.

Initially USS THE SULLIVANS (DDG-68) had a port visit scheduled for Sevastopol, Ukraine. Sevastopol was the largest city in Crimea and a major port on the Black Sea. It was also home to the Russian Navy's Black Sea fleet. Seven years in the future in 2014, Vladimir Putin would annex Crimea and make it part of Russia, igniting a major conflict in Ukraine. In April 2007, U.S. Navy intelligence officials let us know that there was unrest and protests in Sevastopol connected to our scheduled arrival. The Russians had told the locals that Gladys Kravitz was coming and that she was dangerous. Sevastopol was their home turf, and we would not be welcomed as we had been during all our other Black Sea port visits.

Everywhere USS THE SULLIVANS (DDG-68) went in the Black Sea, the Russians would follow. Normally our ship was shadowed by both a Turkish and a Russian frigate. The Russians gave off a creepy sort of Klingon-vibe, like the fictional adversaries of the starship Enterprise in Gene Rodenberry's *Star Trek* series. Russian warships appearing on the horizon and shadowing the U.S. Navy was not unusual. Every time U.S. warships transited the Black Sea, the Russians would follow. In 2007, during both our ventures into the Black Sea, Russian Navy ships trailed USS THE SULLIVANS (DDG-68) but did not try and play chicken with us or violate the nautical rules of the road. They did not send flag signals or talk to us on the radio that I remember. They just followed and stayed a safe distance behind, lurking, listening, and spying. They followed us to Constanta, Romania; Varna, Bulgaria; Bat'umi, Georgia; and Samsun, Turkey. It was the Russians that were playing the role of Gladys Kravitz in the Black Sea, not USS THE SULLIVANS (DDG-68).

The Black Sea was first named by the ancient Greeks, who called it the inhospitable sea. This land-locked body of water was deemed inhospitable because it was difficult to navigate, and the people who lived along its shores did not particularly like the Greeks or Romans who explored the area thousands of years ago. However, both the Romans and Greeks traded and settled along the shores as could be seen in the ruins and architecture throughout the region and heard in the languages spoken. The Black Sea was also littered with well-preserved ancient shipwrecks. Pottery, food items, and art work from these finds were housed in the museums that our crew visited in Constanta and Varna.

The Black Sea is relatively shallow, with an average depth of just over 1,500 meters or about 4,900 feet. As USS THE SULLIVANS (DDG-68) sailed through the center of the Black Sea, we did not see much fishing activity or commercial traffic. In the Mediterranean, Aegean and Adriatic Seas, our ship drivers had to constantly dodge ferries, fishing boats, yachts, sailboats, and cargo vessels. The Black Sea was the opposite of that. It was like the Death Valley of the seven seas. There was not much life or commercial activity in the center for those just passing through like us. No dolphins jumping our bow waves or flying fish soaring across the water, just the Russian and Turkish frigates following methodically in our wake.

U.S. Navy PQS for sewage treatment systems

We also learned that the blackness of the Black Sea's waters was caused by an excess of hydrogen sulfide (H_2S). Hydrogen sulfide drastically reduced the scope and breadth of life outside of bacteria and organisms that could live off sulfur. This was evident to us by the lack of marine mammals and sea birds. Sailors become familiar with the pattern of life on the ocean. In the Black Sea there was no discernable pattern of sea life that we could see. Jacque Cousteau would have been bored here.

U.S. Navy sailors know all too well about hydrogen sulfide, the colorless gas that smells like rotten eggs. While most civilians do not worry about such things, warships with a crew of 300 busy and active sailors generate a lot of human waste. All that poop must be stored onboard in tanks and processed before it can be pumped overboard. Hydrogen sulfide is a byproduct of human waste. Sometimes H_2S gas leaks out of the closed system aboard ship and forms deadly pockets in low lying areas. Sailors are trained to evacuate spaces when they smell rotten eggs. If you remain too long in a space with a high concentration of H_2S gas, the rotten egg smell disappears, which means you are going to pass out and possibly suffocate then die.

H_2S gas emanating from our poop is another hidden danger of the maritime profession and something all USS THE SULLIVANS (DDG-68) sailors had to be trained to detect and evade. Gas-free engineering is the process the Navy uses to ensure ship compartments have the requisite level of oxygen to sustain human life. It is deadly serious business and one of the unclassified, hidden secrets of life aboard a destroyer. Earning a gas-free engineering certification was reserved for very few sailors. It was difficult and time consuming but could be turned into a well-paying civilian career after one's enlistment or Navy career was completed.

USS THE SULLIVANS (DDG-68) engineers repairing piping in 2007

Calcified poop in DDG-68 sewage system 2007

In USS THE SULLIVANS (DDG-68), our engineers noted that excess calcium deposits were overtaking our sewage system plumbing. These calcium deposits constricted sections of pipe and reduced flow and suction, like cholesterol blocking arteries in the human body. The calcium deposits were a major headache and problem because they reduced suction and prompted repeated clogging and spills, which in turn would cause pockets of H_2S gas in certain spaces, including berthing. This was a potential deadly problem for our crew.

THE SULLIVANS engineers methodically inspected sections of the piping and scraped out dozens of putrid calcium deposits from the plumbing system all throughout the ship. This was the dirtiest of jobs but had to be done. I am sure it would have made Mike Rowe very proud. This action significantly improved our sewage system's performance and reduced spillage and H_2S gas pockets. Sometimes *We Stick Together* means cleaning your shipmate's calcified poop out of pipes to keep them happy, healthy, and ready to fight.

Routine work and ship maintenance continued along with cleaning calcified poop out of pipes as USS THE SULLIVANS (DDG-68) steamed across the barren Black Sea. Our voyage plans were scripted and discussed with the Sixth Fleet staff. No audibles could be called about where we were heading or which ports we might approach. This was a high-visibility mission with international press interest. We were being watched by not only the Russians but also our own chain of command, the international media, and repressed and formerly subjugated civilians in places like Ukraine, Georgia, and Moldova. Mistakes in this part of the world had started wars before. An accidental movement of our five-inch gun or performing routine maintenance on our close-in-weapon system (CIWS) mounts could be misinterpreted as hostile intent by our Russian or Turkish minders. We were glad for all the forceful backup from the Office of Naval Intelligence (ONI), the Sixth Fleet staff, and the rest of our chain of command, but when a crew is out on point alone it can certainly feel like there are lots of Gladys Kravitzs peering in your window.

Before we could start our track towards Sevastopol, Sixth Fleet pulled the plug and cancelled our visit. I do not remember the specifics of why the port visit was cancelled–those reasons were likely classified. We were told it was due to local protests and unrest. Sixth Fleet would have to send us somewhere else and that would take us to Samsun.

Map of Turkey and the Black Sea showing the location of Samsun

Samsun was a city of over one million people in central Asia Minor on the Black Sea. It is the site from where Mustafa Kemal, the founder of modern Turkey, began the push for Turkish independence in 1919. In 2007, Samsun was a conservative Sunni Muslim city where the call to prayer happened five times a day and the only bars that served alcohol were in a few major hotels. This was a cultural phenomenon the crew of USS THE SULLIVANS (DDG-68) had not yet experienced on this deployment. As our visit was short notice, there were not a lot of activities planned. Samsun would be for repairs, rest, and recuperation. Samsun was USS THE SULLIVANS' (DDG-68) last port visit in the Black Sea. Our deployment was well past the half-way point. The next segment of our grand adventure would be to begin the nearly 7,000 nautical-mile journey home.

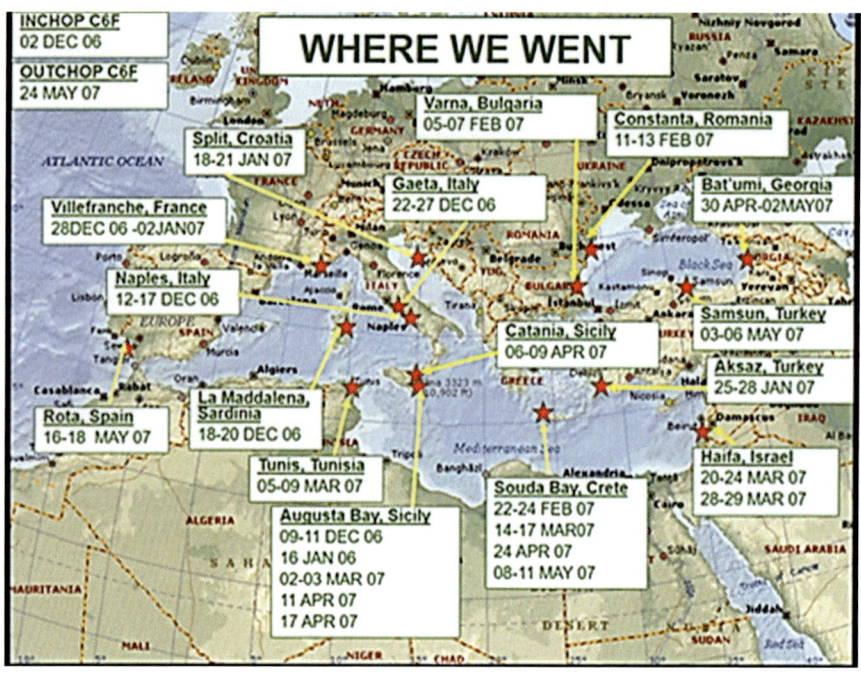

Port visits for USS THE SULLIVANS (DDG-68) while deployed to the Sixth Fleet AOR 2006-2007

Throughout the deployment, THE SULLIVANS crew executed all assigned events and ad hoc tasking on or ahead of time. The men and women of USS THE SULLIVANS (DDG-68) did not miss a mission, event, or evolution due to material, training, or personnel casualties. Additionally after visiting dozens of ports, the crew never had a reportable alcohol-related liberty incident or accident throughout the entire six-month deployment. Morale, battle readiness, and mission focus all remained high eventhough the operational tempo and work-load never let up. Keelhauled played a cruicial role in the ship's success, keeping the crew entertained off duty while fostering good-will and a positive spirit everywhere we went with American rock and roll music.

The Russians never did challenge us directly in the Black Sea. Like Gladys Kravitz, they were just uptight and nosy but never caught us off guard or in a place we where not meant to be. It was down right boring, but that is what success looks like most of the time for U.S. Navy surface warriors. Once in awhile, a U.S. warship will be tasked to launch Tomahawk cruise missiles or fire its main battery in anger, but not this time. USS THE SULLIVANS (DDG-68) stood down the threat and safely steamed in and out of the Black Sea without an international incident. Our bosses were happy but the Russians remained suspicious about our voyages into the Black Sea. Peace is not always sexy and exciting, but it is the happiest outcome for all.

The truth is that the U.S. Navy keeps the world's sea lanes and chokepoints open for international trade and commerce to benefit everyone. This fact is taken for granted by people around the world. U.S. Navy ships deploy to protect and defend our national interests and also to keep the seas free and open from piracy, commerce raiding, and warfare. USS THE SULLIVANS (DDG-68), like all deployable U.S. Navy surface combatants, has routinely patrolled, guarded, and defended the world's shipping lanes and international chokepoints for decades without fanfare. This deployment was nothing new. USS THE SULLIVANS (DDG-68) steamed thousands of miles to keep the peace, build stronger partnerships around the globe, and showcase American values through its *We Stick Together* spirit. This was a worthy endeavor and something our crew could be very proud of for the rest of their lives.

In hindsight THE SULLIVANS' fourth deployment was an overwhelming success and served as a model for all independent deploying ships heading to Sixth Fleet. Sixth Fleet's COMDESRON SIX ZERO stated that THE SULLIVANS crew "embodies their motto, *We Stick Together*. They are focused and sharp … and have prepped the battle space effectively for THE SULLIVANS' relief …"[29]

COMDESRON TWO FOUR, USS THE SULLIVANS (DDG-68) immediate superior in command (ISIC) and home squadron, said,

"THE SULLIVANS' superior performance as an independent deployer to the Sixth Fleet AOR (area of responsibility) contributed to the GWOT (Global War on Terrorism) and maritime security. THE SULLIVANS served as an excellent ambassador during your extensive ports of call … her performance during Exercises Noble Manta and Noble Dina further displayed THE SULLIVANS' warrior spirit. From her war fighting abilities to command climate, no other ship in the squadron has brought so much credit to the United States Navy."[30]

Looking back, THE SULLIVANS' biggest impact during the six-month deployment was in the Black Sea where our military-to-military training

---

29 COMDESRON SIX ZERO unclassified message dated 152057Z MAY 07.
30 COMDESRON TWO FOUR unclassified message dated 042013Z DEC 07.

efforts greatly helped the Romanian Navy, especially with their helicopter operations. THE SULLIVANS' training efforts also positively impacted the Bulgarian and Georgian navies. From Croatia to Israel and up in the Black Sea, THE SULLIVANS trained hard and always had a positive attitude. Our ship's motto—*We Stick Together*—rang true and was used by American ambassadors and sailors alike to demonstrate that the United States was a great ally to have and would be there if and when the need arose. The efforts of the crew showcased America, and what it stands for, and told the story of George, Francis, Joseph, Madison, and Albert Sullivan. They spread the word about what *We Stick Together* meant all around the Mediterranean and Black Seas. They accomplished the mission.

CHAPTER 12

UNDERSTANDING WHAT IT MEANS TO WIN

USS THE SULLIVANS (DDG-68) shooting five inch projectile circa 2006

In the summer of 2006, Will Ferrell, John C. Reilly, and Sacha Baron Cohen starred in the comedy hit *Talladega Nights: The Ballad of Ricky Bobby*. This parody about America and NASCAR resonated with many in the crew of THE SULLIVANS (DDG-68). Ricky Bobby's "rags to riches to rags to good guy" plot made sense and comedic film history. It became part of American popular culture, and always brought smiles to the crew when references or quotes were used from the film. Ricky Bobby was something we could all laugh at and relate to. The plot, characters, and dialogue helped us bridge the generation gap. And although the story was juvenile, this particular comedy struck a chord for many of us in the crew because it contained relatable life lessons, about humility, winning, and being a simple kind of man, echoing the lyrics of one of Keelhauled's mainstay covers for their set list. As luck and timing would have it, *Talledega Nights* coincided perfectly with our deployment and would serve as a ready stowage bin of metaphors, analogies, and mental images to help us all understand what it meant to win.

Nearly a decade later, circa 2016, Chief of Naval Operations (CNO) Admiral John Richardson would talk a lot about winning. On his official podcast, he stated, "I need every member of the Navy Team focused on finding ways to stay ahead of our enemies. All of our energy needs to be focused on getting stronger, faster, smarter, better." CNO Richardson also astutely said, "Warfare is a violent, intellectual contest between thinking and adapting adversaries. The team that can think better and adapt faster will win." [31] His successor, Admiral Michael Gilday, would adopt the tag-line "Be ready to fight and win tonight." This simple phrase would appear everywhere, in official messages, standing orders, and posted on ready room bulkheads. Both Admirals Richardson and Gilday wanted U.S. Navy sailors to be able to win. But what did winning really mean in the post-Cold War, post-9/11 world? What would winning look like? What should we be focusing on every day to be ready to win? These are tough questions that all commanding officers must translate into concrete and tangible actions by their crews, especially when on deployment overseas is some of the roughest maritime neighborhoods of our planet.

---

31 Quotes by ADM J. Richardson, CNO from his official Navy blog circa 2016.

Historically warfare has been viewed as the ultimate zero-sum game; there were always definite winners and clear losers. From the end of World War II to the present day, the U.S. Navy has had the great fortune to be the undisputed champion of the high seas. To steal a line from Ricky Bobby, for over 75 years the U.S. Navy has been "just a big hairy American winning machine," but now the world was changing. Russia, China, Iran, North Korea, Al-Qaeda, and even African pirates were challenging U.S. supremacy on the high seas. At some point in the future some nation, group, or organization will test our ability to fight and win at sea; it is inevitable. The American people have come to expect the U.S. Navy to win, and win "big league" to quote a former de-platformed president. Will we be ready? Are we thinking about this and other problems with the right words and thoughts? Or are we only looking at zero-sum solutions?

Americans love winning, but what does it really mean to win? It is probably best to start with defining the term win. Dictionary.com defines the verb "to win" as "to finish first in a race, contest, or the like."[32] The modern English word "win" comes from the old English word "winnan," which meant to strive, contend, subdue, acquire, and take possession of. The old English word "winnan" was derived from the German word "gewinnen," which, in addition to meaning to win, could mean to carry off, to gain, to extract, and to gain the affection or esteem of. "[33] Today most Americans think of winning in binary terms, but as the etymology of the verb "to win" demonstrates this was not always the case.

---

32 https://www.dictionary.com/browse/win#:~:text=verb%20(used%20without%20object)%2C,adversary%3A%20The%20home%20team%20won. Downloaded June 18, 2021.

33 https://www.etymonline.com/word/win Downloaded June 19, 2021.

Words matter and have a profound impact on how we envision possible outcomes. Although the English language allows for myriad ideas and innovative constructions, by using certain words over and over without focusing on their actual meanings we condition ourselves to think of winning only in zero-sum ways. Today when most of us say or think of the word "win," we anticipate the outcome to be binary; either we win or we lose, there is no middle ground. This is Ricky Bobby thinking "if you ain't first, you're last." Could there be another way to look at winning?

The Battle of Flamborough Head 1779, John Paul Jones defeats HMS SERAPIS

The U.S. Navy was not always the world's most dominant sea power. Our actual beginnings were very humble—just six frigates. In fact, the great American naval hero John Paul Jones could be considered the Ricky Bobby of his day based on his famous quote: "I wish to have no connection with any ship that does not sail fast; for I intend to go in harm's way."[34] Fans of *Talladega Nights: The Ballad of Ricky Bobby* will recognize this quote as a colonial version of Ricky's tag-line "I wanna go fast."

On September 23, 1779, John Paul Jones, commanding a small flotilla of Franco-American ships from USS BONHOMME RICHARD defeated the Royal Navy's HMS SERAPIS and HMS COUNTESS OF SCARBOROUGH in a violent three-hour gun battle off Flamborough Head, England. Many American and British sailors were killed, and John Paul Jone's flagship, BONHOMME RICHARD sank after the battle. John Paul Jones was hailed a hero by the French after this battle. He and his sailors scored a surprising upset victory against the most powerful navy in the world because of their refusal to quit and determination to win.

Comparing John Paul Jones with the fictional Ricky Bobby is heresy and sacrilege to an older generation of officers and chiefs who were taught to venerate the father of the U.S. Navy. But Ricky Bobby is someone that young sailors could instantly relate to and visualize. For many in our young crew, when someone mentioned John Paul Jones, the keyboard and bass player for the rock band Led Zeppelin was more likely to pop into their mind than the dead naval hero of Flamborough Head fame kept in a crypt at the U.S. Naval Academy.

The great Chinese strategist Sun Tzu said "[t]he supreme art of war is to subdue the enemy without fighting." He also advised "Victorious warriors win first and then go to war, while defeated warriors go to war first

---

34 https://www.goodreads.com/quotes/209370-i-wish-to-have-no-connection-with-any-ship-that downloaded September 29, 2021.

and then seek to win."[35] Ricky Bobby demonstrated this theory perfectly on screen when he mindlessly challenges French Formula One star Jean Girard based solely on stereotypical American hubris and pure testosterone-induced zero sum thinking. Ricky ultimately crashes and burns (well, burns in his mind if you know the movie) in spectacular failure because he refused to change his thinking and strategy. He kept on just trying to go fast instead of looking for other ways to win. USS THE SULLIVANS (DDG-68) crew members understood that Ricky Bobby's strategy for winning was flawed. The visual image of his number 26 Chevy, Wonder Bread-sponsored stock car flipping end over end and crashing was a good visual metaphor reminding warriors what happens when you do not do your homework before battle (i.e., ignore the sage advice of Sun Tzu).

Imagine if we could do a round-table discussion with Ricky Bobby, John Paul Jones, and Sun Tzu. What advice would they give us on how to win in changing circumstances? They would all probably start out the conversation by saying that we should start with the end in mind, to clearly understand what it is exactly that we are trying to win. Sun Tzu would most likely tell us that while we prepare for the inevitability of war at sea we should expand our thinking and look for positive-sum outcomes instead of just binary ones so that we can defeat our potential foes without ever firing a shot. John Paul Jones might well advocate changing the game completely and taking the fight to the enemy's backyard while limiting the number of adversaries that can compete against us to better the odds of winning. Ricky Bobby would surely add that just going fast is not enough. He would likely tell us that we need to tame and harness

---

35 https://www.brainyquote.com/authors/sun-tzu-quotes. Sun Tzu downloaded June 19, 2021.

our inner cougar (i.e., keep our emotions in check), and focus on the bigger picture, not just ourselves.

While some THE SULLIVANS crew members might have read or heard of Sun Tzu, most had not. U.S. Navy sailors were familiar with John Paul Jones as the father of the American Navy, but most could not relate to him, as he died in 1792. However, the majority of our crew could relate to Will Ferrell's character Ricky Bobby, as they had all seen the film at least once. The average age of a USS THE SULLIVANS crew member in 2006 was 22 or 23 years old. Ricky Bobby was something they knew and could visualize, while Sun Tzu and John Paul Jones were at best distant historic and unrelatable figures. It was not going to be about just going fast. We would have to maintain our passion and competitive spirit and also use our critical-thinking skills to grasp the bigger picture. *Talladega Nights* would provide the dialogue and images that helped our crew understand what we needed to do as a team. Ricky Bobby would help us win.

MISSION COMPLETED

- RAISED THE BAR FOR ENGAGEMENT IN THE BLACK SEA
- 6th FLEET's SALES REP FOR AIS TV 32 SOFTWARE
- SURFACE WARRIORS & DIPLOMATS
- SHOW CASED SUPERIOR U.S. NAVY INTEGRATED ASW CAPABILITY
- MADE NEW FRIENDS IN THE REGION
- PASSED ON LESSONS LEARNED TO NEXT DEPLOYERS
- NO LIBERTY INCIDENTS
- MET & EXCEEDED ALL MISSION REQUIREMENTS

2007 post-deployment mission completed slide depicting the crew's unclassified achievements

During USS THE SULLIVANS (DDG-68) deployment in late 2006 and early 2007, our crew had to reimagine what it meant to win. Our mission was not a zero-sum game, and there was not going to be a first, second, third, or fourth place when we were done. The U.S. Navy wanted us to quantify our efforts numerically, tracking specific indicators that could be statistically analyzed and monetized. After six months away from homeport, USS THE SULLIVANS (DDG-68) calculated the following:

steamed: 26,250 nautical miles

burned: 2,842,363 gallons of Diesel Fuel Marine (DFM)

used: 2,226,561 gallons of potable H2O

expended: 37,114 rounds of ammunition

participated in: 11 Naval exercises with 10 foreign navies

hosted: 5 VIP receptions for U.S. ambassadors and foreign dignitaries

visited: 24 ports in 11 different countries on 3 separate continents

Did the expenditure of all this time, effort, and resources show that we had won? We believed we had accomplished our mission, and fulfilled our tasking but did we win? Was this the best way to conceptualize what we had accomplished? Many in the crew wanted to know. They wanted to tell their friends and families they had done something meaningful and succeeded. I felt the same way and provided them what I thought was a good response to this question. Here is what I wrote and published in our official plan of the day on April 28, 2007:

With 14 days and a wake up left on our SSG 07-1 deployment some of you maybe already reflecting on how you will answer the question you will inevitably get from your friends and family, "so what was the point of your deployment?" Here are some things you can tell them. The official missions we supported for COMSIXTHFLEET were: intelligence preparation of the environment; theater security cooperation; and maritime domain awareness. We also supported the Global War on Terrorism directly by training with our allies and building bonds of trust which we may have to cash at a later date. You also sailed in support of Operation Active Endeavour, the only NATO Article V operation ever conducted.... the most important thing we did on deployment was showcase America, what it stands for and tell the story of George, Francis, Joseph, Madison, and Albert Sullivan. We spread the word about what We Stick Together means all around the Mediterranean and Black Seas... .tell your loved ones you served your country during the Global War on Terror by sacrificing your time and talent so that they could be safe, free, and pursue happiness.

This is how I described winning. It was not a binary answer. We did our best and succeeded at every task, evolution, and training opportunity that came our way. We had our ups and downs, but in the end we successfully completed what we set out to do. We returned home safely with lots of stories to tell. We had won. There would be no victory parades, treasure, or tribute. *We Stick Together* meant successfully accomplishing the mission with humility and grace. Our deployment was not meant to be a race but an exercise in vigilance and a test of character.

CHAPTER 13

STAYING ALERT AND BEING VIGILANT

March 2007 Haifa, Israel CDR Tony Parisi onboard INS LAHAV, SA'AR 5 Corvette

During my two tours in command of U.S. warships, USS ZEPHYR (PC-8) and USS THE SULLIVANS (DDG-68), our crews never fired our guns in anger, nor did we face enemies at sea such as our forefathers had in World War II, Korea, or Vietnam. In the post-Cold War, post-9/11 world, there were enemies but none that challenged USS THE SULLIVANS

(DDG-68) directly, at least that we were aware of. [36] In 2006 and 2007, we spent six months deployed, training and working with foreign navies. While these missions were hard work and rewarding, they were not combat.

USS THE SULLIVANS (DDG-68) did have the privilege of participating in Exercise Noble Dina 2007 with the Israeli Navy. Noble Dina is an annual maritime security exercise conducted with Israel in the eastern Mediterranean Sea. Israel takes this exercise very seriously and uses it to train and improve their Navy and maritime capabilities. In 2007, the Noble Dina exercise focused on anti-submarine warfare (ASW); helicopter operations; visit, board, search, and seizure training (VBSS); and search and rescue operations (SAR). The crew of USS THE SULLIVANS (DDG-68) also used Israeli Navy shore-based damage control trainers and hosted Israeli Navy personnel on our ship for cross-training. The overall aim of the U.S. Navy's participation in Noble Dina was to strengthen the relationship between the Israeli defense forces and the U.S. military so as to facilitate future security cooperation activities should they be necessary.

During our time in Haifa and training with the Israeli Navy, I became good friends with the commanding officer of INS LAHAV, a Sa'ar V corvette. I learned that "lahav" means blade in Hebrew. Names matter, and this Israeli ship's name reflected its purpose—to be a close-in defensive weapon that was sharpened and ready for combat. Captain Ben (I am using a pseudonym to protect his true identity), as I will call him, was

---

36 In January 2000 during a brief stop for fuel in Aden, Yemen, Al-Qaeda terrorists made an attempt to blow up USS THE SULLIVANS (DDG-68) with a bomb-laden suicide boat. The attack was aborted but re-attempted and successful in October 2000 when USS COLE (DDG-67) was blown up and nearly sunk. Seventeen U.S. Navy sailors died and many more were injured in that attack.

a combat veteran who had seen action at sea against real combatants during Israel's occupation of Lebanon and the fighting with Hezbollah. Ben took me on a tour of LAHAV and showed me the exact spot where a C802 missile launched by Hezbollah struck the flight deck of LAHAV's sister ship INS HANIT.

Photos of damage to INS HANIT [37]

37 https://www.ynetnews.com/articles/0,7340,L-3458845,00.html. Photos and story by Hanan Greenberg, published October 11, 2007.

Flight deck on INS HANIT after C802 missile strike[38]

This attack happened on July 14, 2006, only eight months before USS THE SULLIVANS (DDG-68) arrived in Haifa. We walked the flight deck and he spoke with passion and sadness of how the missile hit the aft part of the ship and ignited a class bravo fire (oil and chemical fire). INS HANIT's crew courageously fought the fire and prevented further damage to the ship but took casualties. Ben explained how INS HANIT lost sailors in this attack, and how the ship was caught off guard.

INS HANIT and INS LAHAV, the Sa'ar V ship class, were built in the United States and looked like a mini-version of the Arleigh Burke-class DDG in many respects. At the time of the attack, The SA'AR V's were the most advanced warships homeported in the Eastern Mediterranean. Their air defense systems and electronic warning suite were modern and reliable and more than capable of downing a subsonic cruise missile-if the systems were fully readied and HANIT's operators had remained alert and

38 Ibid.

vigilant. INS HANIT's crew had no intelligence or warning that Hezbollah was even capable of firing anti-ship missiles. On July 14, 2006, HANIT's crew, like the crews of USS STARK (FFG-31) on May 17, 1987, and USS COLE (DDG-67) on October 12, 2000, was caught completely off guard. HANIT's anti-air weapon (AAW) systems were not ready, and her watch standers were not alert when Hezbollah fighters launched C802s missiles that night. When a ship's crew is not expecting an attack, and not ready to fight back, no amount of high technology can protect the ship.

USS STARK (FFG-31) hit by two Exocet missiles in the Persian Gulf May 17, 1987

*USS COLE (DDG-67) hit by Al-Qaeda suicide-bomb
boat in Aden, Yemen October 12, 2000*

USS STARK (FFG-31) was a Mayport based Oliver Hazard Perry-class fast frigate which was struck by two French-made Exocet missiles launched from an Iraqi aircraft during the Iran-Iraq War while patrolling in the Persian Gulf on May 17, 1987. Thirty-seven U.S. sailors died and twenty-one more were wounded. USS COLE (DDG-68) is a Norfolk based Arleigh Burke-class destroyer. On October 12, 2000, the ship was attacked by Al-Qaeda terrorists while refueling in Aden, Yemen. Seventeen U.S. sailors died and thirty-seven were injured during this attack.

The crew of USS THE SULLIVANS (DDG-68) was very familiar with the details of both of these incidents. Our war council had read the lessons learned and analyzed the case studies on both these unexpected attacks. Many of us knew sailors that served on these vessels, and had participated in remembrance ceremonies honoring our fellow fallen surface warfare warriors. USS THE SULLIVANS (DDG-68) crew members drove past the STARK Memorial everyday while in homeport, as it served as the focal point of Memorial Park at Naval Station Mayport. The concrete pillar and brass plaque with the 37 names was a constant reminder of the danger we all faced every time we took in the lines and headed to sea.

The night of July 14, 2006, Hezbollah launched a volley of two or three C802 Chinese-designed Iranian-supplied anti-ship missiles from a shore-based launcher somewhere near Beirut, Lebanon. One of the missiles struck HANIT as described by Ben and killed four Israeli soldiers (the Israelis call all their military personnel soldiers). Another missile struck a Cambodian merchant vessel named MOONLIGHT, causing it to sink. The attack happened around 8:30 PM local time as HANIT was patrolling about 10 nautical miles (nm) from the coast of Beirut. HANIT's mission at the time was to blockade the coast and prevent weapons and personnel from reaching or leaving Lebanon. Ben stated that HANIT's daily focus was on close in anti-terrorism force protection (ATFP) and visit, board, search, seizure (VBSS) missions.

Like in the attacks on USS STARK (FFG-31) and USS COLE (DDG-67), there was no intelligence or warning provided to HANIT's crew prior to Hezbollah's missile strike. STARK, COLE, and HANIT were all warships performing real-world missions in or near combat zones. Their crews were all well trained and qualified for their positions. None of these ships expected to be attacked in the manner that they were. They just did not see the attacks coming. So how could this happen to modern, high-tech warships manned by well-trained crews while on real-world deployments?

STARK, COLE, and HANIT proved the effectiveness of the surprise attack. We must assume that our enemies have read the lessons learned from Pearl Harbor in 1941 and the destruction of the Twin Towers and the Pentagon in 2001. Sudden and unexpected attacks on unsuspecting targets generally work. Preventing these types of strikes requires the defenders to remain alert and vigilant at all times. The enemy is waiting for us to let our guard down. The bad guys get to choose how, when, and where they attack and only have to be successful one time to win. The odds will always be in their favor, and will increase if we are not willing to do what it takes to remain ready to fight. This has been the truth throughout history and is not going to change. That is just the way warfare works.

As I toured LAHAV that day in Haifa, I realized that similar attacks would be attempted in the future because they were cost-effective and provided lots of propaganda for our enemies. Hezbollah and other groups were learning how to score hits against the world's most advanced navies. This was cause for concern. USS THE SULLIVANS (DDG-68) would have to remain vigilant and ready for anything as we were not likely to be warned prior to such an attack. Warfare in the post-Cold War, post-9/11 world equalled unseen enemies and innovative new attack methods. Hunter S. Thompson was right when he said, "There is no such thing as paranoia. Your worst fears can come true at any moment."[39]

That day onboard INS LAHAV stuck with me for the rest of the deployment and ever since. USS THE SULLIVANS (DDG-68) and the rest of the U.S. Navy needed to be ready to fight tonight or any night. Maintaining the right level of alertness and vigilance all the time would be a Herculean task. Had INS HANIT been ready for the attack that night, they would

---

39 https://www.brainyquote.com/topics/paranoia-quotes. Downloaded June 22, 2021.

have had 60 seconds or less to shoot or not shoot. Even with the most modern technological anti-air warfare systems, subsonic cruise missiles, even crude Chinese-designed ones, fly at around 9 miles a minute. Our operators would have to be alert and vigilant every time they were on watch. We would need to use our critical thinking skills and hypothesize where we were weakest and prepare for attacks in those areas. Training and learning could never stop. *We Stick Together* meant we had to get better at the things we cared about.

CHAPTER 14

HOW TO GET BETTER AT DOING
THE THINGS YOU CARE ABOUT

CDR Tony Parisi, USN conducting M-60 machine gun practice circa 2006 at sea

How does an individual, team, or crew get better at doing things they care about? Whether you want to learn a foreign language, play guitar, shoot a gun, or get a ship ready for battle, getting better at doing things takes dedicated effort, energy, and resources. Commanding officers of U.S. warships spend the vast majority of their command tours trying to get their crews ready for battles they hope never happen. Commanding officers are also taught and trained to leave their ships and crews better than they found them. In 2006, this was my focus during my command tour in USS THE SULLIVANS (DDG-68).

The "science of learning" and "the revolution in training" were the hot buzzwords in both civilian and military training circles in 2006. The U.S. Navy was going all in on computer simulators and software to enhance learning and training ashore and at sea. Computer simulation meant cost savings for the Navy's school houses, training establishment, and fleet. Over time the Navy would find the right mix between electronic simulation and actual training at sea, but in the euphoria of this latest revolution in training entire school houses and curricula were being moved to CD ROM and laptops. This was especially true for basic surface warfare training for junior officers.[40]

In 2006 the Navy shore establishment taught and trained students using many different methods. I specifically remember learning and training via:

- Powerpoint slides with and without instructors
- Seminar sessions-question and answer periods on a certain topic
- Reading, mostly off a computer screen
- Trainers: electronic simulators for ship driving, warfighting, and familiarization
- Firefighting training using propane instead of diesel fuel as the source of fire
- Field trips: underway and to certain locations (i.e., Navy Boot Camp Great Lakes, IL)

---

40 In 2003 the surface warfare basic training course for division officers headed to their first ships was cut and moved to CD ROM. Newly minted Ensigns reported to their first ships and were given CD ROMs to learn at their own pace.

- Movie clips and video tape
- Interactive CD ROMs and online training
- Talk throughs walk throughs
- Multiple-choice and essay question tests

I tried to learn as much as I could from each of these information delivery methods. My preferred way of learning, however, was for a proven subject matter expert (i.e., a human being) to show me the right way to do something and then to do as many reps and sets as time would allow. I loved being a student and relished my time in college, navy training commands, and graduate school. Learning was a hobby as well as part of my professional development.

The most effective training I received enroute to USS THE SULLIVANS (DDG-68) was at the Surface Warfare Officers School (SWOS) Command in Newport, Rhode Island, and the Aegis Training and Readiness Center (ATRC) in Dahlgren, Virginia. SWOS and ATRC Dahlgren's simulators were the best money could buy, but what really made these two locations great places to learn were real experienced instructors. Both SWOS and ATRC had cadres of subject matter experts, who had been there and done that. They knew what right looked like and were able to convey their knowledge professionally in ways that could be understood and then practiced. In addition to the instructors, my fellow students were all highly motivated to learn as well. Their professional curiosity and competitive nature meant learning never stopped. At lunch, at the gym, on the golf course, questions, dialogue, and comprehension continued.

The U.S. Navy is largely an on-the-job training organization. Historically sailors would receive basic military instruction at boot camp and then go on to A and C schools for their formalized rate training. When they arrived on their ships, they would apprentice and learn on the job before someone would formally qualify them for a position, watch, or key leadership role. This system has worked well for the U.S. Navy and continues to the present day. Computer simulation that can augment this process is value added but can never entirely replace live training at sea.

Continued self-improvement is something the U.S. Navy desires and pushes sailors to achieve. Gaining a high level of knowledge fosters a questioning attitude and the ability to provide forceful backup to one's shipmates. Individual training must occur before effective team training can begin. Navy senior leaders understand that a sailor's mind is their most important and effective weapon. They are tasked to continually fill and replenish their individual knowledge buckets and then pull from them to enhance their team and crew. Apart from actual combat, training is the most important activity we do in the U.S. Navy.

*U.S. Naval Aviation flight hour patches: P-3C Orion
7,000 hours, F-14 Tomcat 2,000 hours*

Whether it is warfighting, weightlifting, or water polo, whatever it is one is trying to get better at requires continuous focus, practice, and learning. Malcolm Gladwell's best-seller *Outliers: The Story of Success* describes what he termed the 10,000-hour rule. Gladwell stated that in any cognitively complex field, there is a consistent pattern of excellence which requires 10,000 hours of practice. This equates to a period of ten years if one does approximately four hours of dedicated practice a day for 250 days on average per year. Mr. Gladwell made a lot of money with his book simply restating what U.S. Navy aviators had known and been doing for years. Flying aircraft for hundreds and thousands of hours equated to excellence and expertise. Naval aviators proudly wear their flight-hour patches on their flight suits and jackets for everyone to see.

While practice certainly can lead to improvement, bad practice will not. Sailors need to know what right looks like. To get better at the things we care about, we need to continually learn, improve, and strive towards a higher performance benchmark. When we reach that goal, we must set another and do it all over again. Like in the ancient myth where Zeus made Sisyphus continuously push a boulder up a hill, Navy training never stops. And for some sailors this does feel like eternal damnation, but for those who embrace it continual learning and performance enhancement brings much satisfaction. The continual push for excellence is indeed a noble cause, especially when it is done to secure the blessings of liberty, democracy, and happiness for friends, family, and our shipmates.

Good training is easy to embrace but assessment masquerading as training is a tough pill to swallow. Some navy training organizations seemed to drift towards collecting data and compiling metrics rather than showing sailors what right looks like. No one likes this brand of training. Inspections and assessment are necessary, but they are not training. Inspections performed by real subject matter experts are great learning opportunities but can feel painful in the moment. In time, learning and training can become a rewarding and pleasurable activity if long-term knowledge acquisition is desired. I certainly felt this way and tried hard to convey this sentiment to the crew of USS THE SULLIVANS (DDG-68). I believed that learning and training should not be tedious and dreaded. Training can be fun.

USS THE SULLIVANS (DDG-68) 12 gauge shotgun qualification at sea 2007

During THE SULLIVANS 2006-2007 deployment, we trained a lot. One area of training most of the crew enjoyed was shooting. Whether it was small arms, five-inch guns, torpedoes, or missiles, our crew enjoyed firing their weapon systems in peace-time. Perhaps it brought cathartic release or maybe it was the element of danger involved with live weapons shoots, I am not sure, but I do remember our crew thoroughly enjoying any and all training that culminated with rounds going down range, myself included. USS THE SULLIVANS (DDG-68) was a warship after all. We took pride in our profession and worked hard at being both professional mariners and warriors. USS COLE (DDG-67), 9/11, and the Global War on Terrorism were still fresh in our minds in 2006. We knew we had to be ready and stay vigilant, for as George Washington had stated over two centuries ago, "To be prepared for war is one of the most effectual means of preserving peace."[41] Our sailors were not looking for a fight but would be ready should one come our way.

Training continued every day throughout my time on USS THE SULLIVANS (DDG-68). We never stopped learning or training. We grew our own subject matter experts over time who would go on to train the next generation of sailors. When learning and training are valued by selfless leaders and passionately pursued, everyone benefits. Training sailors was something I thoroughly enjoyed in USS THE SULLIVANS (DDG-68). Educating and training Sailors would become my main focus for the rest of my Navy career and beyond.

---

41 Quotations of George Washington, Applewood Books, Carlisle, MA 2003, p.7.

CHAPTER 15

INCIDENTS, ACCIDENTS, AND ACCOUNTABILITY

NCIS Coin from Mayport, FL field office

U.S. Navy standard issue M-9 Beretta 9mm pistol

Not every day in command of USS THE SULLIVANS (DDG-68) was sunshine and rainbows. Things went wrong and mistakes happened. And when they did, anger, pain, sadness, and stress also came along for the ride. One incident stands out and remains painfully etched in my mind. It involved a stolen U.S. Navy Beretta M9 pistol. This single incident prompted investigations, root-cause analyses, rigid new protocols, off-ship reports, and above all else holding people accountable. Things go wrong in every ship. Holding people accountable for their actions and their inaction is the foundation of command at sea. It was not fun, and I took no pleasure in doing it, but it was necessary for good order and discipline.

On October 6, 2006, I received a phone call from an Naval Criminal Investigative Service (NCIS) agent who proceeded to tell me that one of my sailors was in custody after threatening to shoot his roommate. The NCIS agent then said that this Sailor had stolen a Beretta M9 pistol from our ship and used it during this offense. The sailor confessed to the crime and stealing the weapon and was being held at Naval Air Station Jacksonville's brig prior to court martial. This is not the kind of phone call I ever expected or wanted to receive. I remember calling my commodore and explaining what I had just learned. He remained calm and listened carefully as I told him that we would send the required Navy special incident operational report (aka OPREP-3 NAVY BLUE) message as soon as possible.[42] I remember him directing me to conduct a thorough investigation and hold the right people accountable. I agreed but had no idea how that would turn out or how difficult it would be.

---

42 The U.S. Navy OPREP-3 reporting system is a formatted message and voice reporting system which provides the initial information to U.S. Navy authorities about an incident of high U.S. Navy interest.

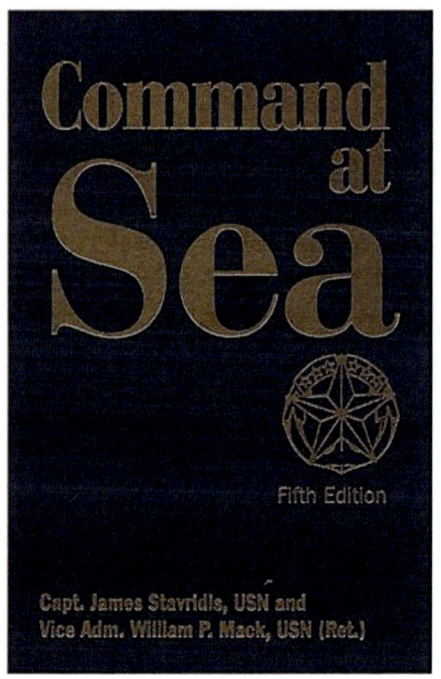

U.S. Navy official command at sea text book

U.S. Navy command at sea pin

U.S. Navy Regulations state that "the responsibility of the commanding officer for his or her command is absolute," and that "the authority of the commanding officer is commensurate with his or her responsibility … whether for success or failure."[43] Failure is not something most people like to admit. In the fall of 2006, USS THE SULLIVANS (DDG-68) had a solid reputation on the waterfront for being a well-performing warship. This incident damaged that reputation and called into question all our routine procedures, specifically the veracity of our small arms inventories. As the commanding officer, I owned that and had to fix it. This was my failure.

In the U.S. Navy, accountability and integrity go hand in hand. When a sailor is responsible for other sailors, equipment, or an evolution, they are also accountable for what happens. As the commanding officer of USS THE SULLIVANS (DDG-68), I was ultimately responsible and accountable for the safety and security of my crew and all the equipment entrusted to our care. I assigned an investigating officer in writing and empowered him to find out the full story and truth of what went wrong. I wanted to know how a sailor stole a pistol from a locked safe and walked it right off the ship. Why didn't our weekly inventory of small arms detect that we had a weapon missing? We needed to fix this process and make our small arms weapons inventories air-tight again. I also wanted to make sure something like this could never happen again in USS THE SULLIVANS (DDG-68).

The investigation uncovered that the sailor in question routinely worked and stood watch on our bridge. He had noticed that there was an M-9 pistol and some loaded magazines in the safe on the bridge. He also

---

43 Capt. James Stavridis, USN and Vice Adm William P. Mack, USN (Ret), Command at Sea, Fifth Edition, U.S. Naval Institute, Annapolis, Maryland, 1999, p.1.

learned the combination to the safe. This weapon was stored in this safe because of a previous policy and practice that was put in place long before I took command. A new department head and other new sailors in the chain of command had since taken charge of the weapons department, but they were not aware that this pistol was not part of the weekly small arms inventory. I had been in command for five months and did not realize that we had a pistol locked in the safe on the bridge. I had been a combat systems officer and commanding officer in previous tours. I knew the rules regarding small arms weapons inventories and the custody chain of pistols. The weapon in question should never have been left in the safe on the bridge. It also should have been part of a weekly small arms inventory, but it was not. When it went missing, no one noticed until I received a phone call from NCIS. Our investigation also uncovered that our weekly and monthly small arms inventories were not being conducted with the focus they should have been, where each weapon was physically sighted and its serial number checked. This news came as a shock to many of us and made us realize we were not as good as we thought we were.

The sailor that took the pistol from the safe went against everything that *We Stick Together* meant. He not only stole government property but also violated the trust and bond with his shipmates. Had this sailor turned the pistol over or pointed out to someone in the chain of command that there was a duty weapon forgotten about on the bridge, he could have helped fix the problem. Instead he chose to become a felon by smuggling the weapon past the quarterdeck watch and off the ship by stuffing it deep inside his seabag. The sailor had the pistol only a short while before he threatened his roommate with it and was arrested. In the end this Sailor was convicted of his crime at court martial, dishonorably discharged, and sentenced to a long stretch in the brig. Justice was served, but accountability for the break-down in procedural compliance that led to this incident in USS THE SULLIVANS (DDG-68) still needed to be addressed.

What we learned was that many in the chain of command believed proper inventories were being conducted as per U.S. Navy regulations and instructions. The weekly small arms inventories were conducted and there were signed copies to demonstrate this, but no one had caught this glaring error. Somehow the pistol that had been kept on the bridge was not part of the inventory, and no one up the chain of command had verified that it had not been returned to the armory. Our small arms inventory process had drifted into complacency and lack of attention to detail over time. New people came and went but no one up the chain of command, including me, took the time to make sure that one of our most basic processes was operating effectively.

From what we learned we immediately instituted daily small arms weapons inventories, where each weapon was physically inspected and verified by serial number by a qualified subject matter expert. The department head would verify that this had been done and then bring me the reports every day. This process was painful and caused hundreds of man-hours of extra work, but it was necessary. The department head, division officer, and chief petty officer of the division responsible were all held accountable. They all went through a formal disciplinary review process and ended up with letters of instruction and other disciplinary measures. This one incident caused much pain for many in the crew. In time when we were sure that our new process was in place and the right level of attention to detail was being given, our small arms inventories went back to the required weekly verifications. We also made sure there were new foolproof protocols in place for any weapon that left the armory. The stolen pistol had taught us all a valuable yet painful lesson.

There were other evolutions, procedures, and sailors that went bad in my tenure in USS THE SULLIVANS (DDG-68). After the stolen pistol incident, unfortunately, none of them came as such a big shock. People are flawed and make mistakes. The overwhelming majority of U.S. Navy sailors want to succeed and just need to know what right looks like first. When a focused subject matter expert shows them what right looks like and then holds them accountable for their actions, or inaction, success is a natural byproduct. Accountability is not a one and done event. It had to be purposefully injected into everything we did in USS THE SULLIVANS (DDG-68) going forward.

Human beings make mistakes. As the English poet Alexander Pope proclaimed in 1711, "To err is human; to forgive, divine."[44] Human error is a contributing factor in every Navy accident and incident. Mitigating human error is the responsibility of all sailors. The U.S. Navy uses SSOPP and formal courses like Bridge Resource Management (BRM) to address and focus on how to mitigate human error at sea. The possibility of human error increases when stress, complacency, distraction, fatigue, pressure, and other factors degrade a sailor's ability to focus and think critically.

Reducing human error saves money and time and increases battle readiness. The U.S. Navy, along with the private industry, continues to use technology and automation to reduce the possibility of human error. In Japan, this concept is called poka-yoke, or mistake-proofing. Poka-yoke

---

44 https://www.phrases.org.uk/meanings/to-err-is-human.html. Quote by Alexander Pope originally from his "An Essay on Criticism, Part II," 1711. Downloaded June 25, 2021.

is "the use of any automatic device or method that either makes it impossible for an error to occur or makes the error immediately obvious once it has occurred."[45] For example, when the microwave oven was first invented, it was possible to turn on the magnetron and microwave with the door open. This was dangerous and potentially fatal. Building microwaves with switches that prevented the magnetron from radiating when the door was open was a poka-yoke. A more pejorative Navy phrase for this idea was sailor-proofing.

Technology and mechanical poka-yoke cannot stop all human errors, especially aboard ships. Whenever and wherever a sailor must perform a complex action, stand a watch, or turn a wrench, human error can and will occur. In this regard, USS THE SULLIVANS (DDG-68) was no better or no worse than other ships on the waterfront. Sometimes ego, pride, and passion can disguise the truth regarding potential disasters, as senior leaders aboard HMS TITANIC and at the nuclear power station in Chernobyl tragically learned. Understanding where we needed more poka-yoke and sailor-proofing became the new focus of USS THE SULLIVANS (DDG-68) for the next few months. We had to make sure we had the basics right before our upcoming deployment.

In hindsight I realize I was too trusting and naïve when I took command of USS THE SULLIVANS (DDG-68). I never expected to have problems with weapons inventories or ammunition counts because, foolishly, I thought I knew what right looked like in these matters. I trusted the signed inventories and reports delivered to me, thinking they had been done the same way I had done them so many years ago. There is an old saying in the Navy that warns you get what you inspect not what you

---

45 https://asq.org/quality-resources/mistake-proofing. Definition of poka-yoke downloaded June 25, 2021.

expect. NCIS and the stolen M-9 forced us to relearn this lesson the hard way. Holding people that you trust accountable is difficult, especially the first time. It gets easier after that because everyone realizes it is the right thing to do. The continuous pursuit of self-improvement and excellence demands everyone to do their job correctly. We all had to inspect as well as trust. It was my job to set the example. I would try harder and do better going forward. Vigilance and accountability are necessary, especially when people's lives are at stake. *We Stick Together* meant we must hold everyone accountable.

CHAPTER 16

DON'T BE MAGELLAN

Portrait of Ferdinand Magellan

Ferdinand Magellen's voyage around the world 1519

Ferdinand Magellan (1480–1521) was a Portuguese explorer who sailed for Spain and discovered the passage through Patagonia (modern-day Chile and Argentina) to the Pacific Ocean. Glory, fame, and riches drove Magellan to betray his native Portugal and sail for Charles V, the Holy Roman Emperor, Archduke of Austria, and the king of Spain. Magellan was a tough, hard-nosed captain. He would have been considered a screamer and tyrant by modern surface warfare officers. By all accounts, Magellan was also an intelligent, strong leader and an extremely competent captain and navigator.

A fleet of ships under Magellan's command left Seville, Spain, in 1519 and sailed west across the Atlantic, looking for a way to reach the Spice Islands near modern-day Indonesia. Magellan eventually made landfall near Rio de Janeiro, Brazil. From there he and his men sailed south, looking for an inland waterway through the continent of South America. Despite much hardship, mutiny, scurvy, and horrendous weather, Magellan found the way through Patagonia. The Strait of Magellan was named in his honor. Later, after crossing the Pacific Ocean, Magellan was killed at Mactan Island in the Philippines by natives. Although he achieved fame by launching the first voyage to circumnavigate the globe, Ferdinand Magellan never completed the journey, was stabbed to death, and died alone in the surf.

Map of Strait of Magellan, South America

Photo from actual Strait of Magellan in Chile

Although I am proud of my Portuguese heritage, I never wanted to be Magellan. When I was in command of USS ZEPHYR (PC-8), we transited the Strait of Magellan. It was a cold and awe-inspiring voyage with no navigational aids through hair-pin turns, dark green waters, and rocky cliffs resembling the fjords of Norway. To this day I wonder how Magellan and his team figured out their way through that wind-swept maze with no charts or GPS. Conducting hydrographic surveys and exploring uncharted territory was just not my thing. I did not want to be Magellan.

This would become my mantra in command of USS THE SULLIVANS (DDG-68). What I meant by this was I had no desire to volunteer to be the first Arleigh Burke class DDG to go to a new pier, port, or city where no other U.S. Navy ship had been before. Although we were confident in our ability to navigate anywhere safely, we understood the risks and dangers associated with voyage planning in the least-visited parts of the globe. It always seemed to be high-risk with little gain for those trying to go pier side with a large pressurized rubber sonar dome and a draft of 32 feet or 10 meters. USS THE SULLIVANS (DDG-68) was designed to be a blue water warship, not a hydrographic research vessel. Ferdinand Magellan was a great explorer and navigator who was interested in riches, fame, and glory. His voyage of discovery did not end well, so there was no need to repeat it.

When USS THE SULLIVANS (DDG-68) deployed in support of the Commander, U.S. Sixth Fleet (aka COMSIXTHFLT) in 2006, most of our ship drivers, the junior officers who would drive the ship, had never deployed to the Mediterranean or the Black Seas. For them, every port visit and pier landing would be a journey of discovery. USS THE SULLIVANS (DDG-68) was going to visit places not well travelled by Sixth Fleet ships, such as Batumi, Varna, Constanta, and Samsun. Not being Magellan meant we needed to do deep research on each one of these locations. We would not be able to send a scouting team ahead like Magellan did in his day, but we could scour the Navy lessons learned database and the internet and ask the host nation to provide the resources we needed to finalize our voyage plans. The devil was in the details, so find the devil before he finds us.

In USS THE SULLIVANS (DDG-68) our navigation team and conning officers were expected to do a deep dive and prepare a brief with visual images of the pier and port we would visit. I wanted them to become subject matter experts and know where they were going and not guess like Magellan and his crew had to do. This was my minimum standard for every sea and anchor brief. To excel as professional mariners, everyone was encouraged to exceed the minimum standard, and most did. Everyone on our navigation team needed to be able to look out the window and clearly understand where we were going and how we would maneuver the ship to arrive safely. The stakes were high. If we touched bottom or hit something, it was game over for everyone's Naval career; so don't be Magellan.

Varna was just such a port. After entering the Black Sea, USS THE SULLIVANS (DDG-68) was tasked with a mission by COMSIXTHFLT to visit Varna and conduct multi-national joint exercises with the Bulgarian and Romanian navies. Bulgaria and Romania were new members to the NATO alliance. Their navies had not worked with one another since before the Cold War, nor had they ever worked with NATO ships. Our mission was focused on training and diplomacy. Romania and Bulgaria needed the U.S. Navy to serve as a bridge between them before they could start working with one another.

The Bulgarian Navy had old Soviet-era Riga and Koni class warships. The Romanian Navy used more modern former British Type 22 class frigates. Getting these vintage vessels underway and establishing functional communications with us would be a challenge all by itself. Creating a meaningful set of at-sea exercises that did not consume too many precious resources (i.e., fuel, ordnance, and flight hours) would take creative thinking and focused investigative analysis. USS THE SULLIVANS (DDG-68) was tasked with a Magellan mission, which was to be the first U.S./NATO warship to conduct a multi-national naval exercise with both Romania and Bulgaria.

We did not volunteer for this mission, but we would be the first to try it. We would do our best to make it a success and pass on our lessons learned so that those that came after us could build on what we discovered in order to strengthen the NATO alliance. We also planned to assess what type of individual and team training each ship needed and would provide what we could with our available subject matter experts. We had to manage Bulgarian, Romanian, and Sixth Fleet's expectations as we constructed our plan. We did not want to be like Magellan and go down in the history books as the first U.S. Navy warship to attempt this mission and then die in the surf, figuratively speaking. We were determined to succeed and were not interested in riches, fame, and glory. We were focused on doing our job well.

Before we could formulate exercise planning with two new NATO navies, we first had to arrive safely in port. Looking at the paper charts we had at the time, it appeared theoretically possible to enter the harbor and spin the ship around to go starboard side towards the pier, but it would not be easy. We had to consider the wind, current, pier loading, and the ability of the pilot to maneuver our ship, which he was not familiar with.

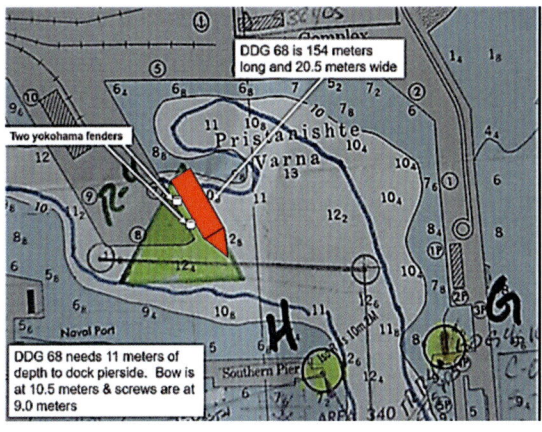

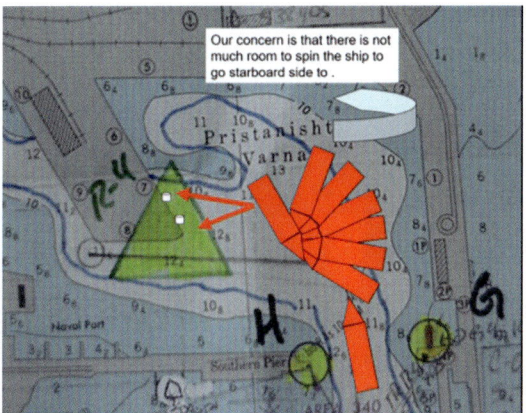

Varna, Bulgaria harbor nautical charts from February 2007

After much planning we pulled together a strategy using operational risk management to minimize the danger. We created no-go criteria as follows:

1. Winds greater than 15 knots

2. Vessel at pier 8 overhanging eastern edge—where our bow has to go

3. Poor visibility

4. Need at least two tugs

5. Adequate turning space—no ships at adjacent piers

6. At least two Yokohama fenders in place

If one or more of these no-go criteria were met, we would make other arrangements or anchor out. Our team had made a solid plan. We would all be rested and focused for entering port. Our brief had pictures of the pier, the most recent depth soundings, and everything we could think of to permit safe passage into port.

USS THE SULLIVANS (DDG-68) in port Varna, Bulgaria February 2007

The morning of February 5, 2007, with country clearance and permission to enter Bulgarian territorial waters in hand, we proceeded to the pilot pick-up point. Our no-go criteria were not met, which meant it was a go for entering port. The winds were low and the weather was sunny and calm. We had all done our homework. This would be our first time visiting Bulgaria. The bridge team was ready and the entering port checklist was complete.

When the pilot arrived onboard, our command master chief brought him to the pilot house. I shook his hand, and we began to discuss how we would enter Varna harbor and spin the ship around. The pilot had a laptop with a portable GPS device plugged in. He was prepared and confident and spoke fluent English. He also said that he had three tugs available and that spinning the ship in the harbor would be easy. His confidence was contagious, and his demeanor was friendly and focused. This is how all pilots and U.S. Navy sailors should be: prepared, professional, and polite.

The Bulgarian pilot's skill exceeded our expectations. He was a competent mariner with years of experience and a deep level of knowledge about the currents, wind, and piers in Varna harbor. He listened well as we explained how our gas turbine-driven twin controllable, reversible pitch propellers functioned. From his body language, attitude, and focus it was evident he wanted to learn about the shiphandling characteristics of Arleigh Burke class destroyers as he knew he would have to dock similar U.S. Navy warships here in Varna in the coming years.

The pilot took the time to explain exactly what he was going to do before he did it and then translated his orders from English to Bulgarian to the three tug boat masters, who did exactly as he ordered. In the U.S. Navy we train watchstanders to give orders not requests, as this can lead to confusion and misunderstandings, especially in times of crisis. This pilot understood this concept and put it into practice by way of a hand-held VHF radio. The tug masters all answered his orders with prompt positive responses. Our bridge watch team could comprehend this without understanding one word of Bulgarian by the tone of the orders and responses between the pilot and the tugs. Everyone remained calm, cool, and even tempered. When a person does his job well it drives others to do the same, causing a positive chain reaction that most often results in success.

The pilot and tugs smoothly spun our nearly 9,000-ton destroyer around in the small Soviet-era constructed basin in Varna harbor, where we were designated to dock, and then pushed us gently into position against two large black Yokahama fenders. The entire evolution lasted less than 20 minutes and was one of the safest and smoothest moorings of the dozens we had made in more frequently used NATO ports. Our pilot had grown up and lived under communism, but his nation's previous ideology did not impede his level of knowledge and professional mariner skills. He was clearly the best, most prepared docking pilot we had seen in the Black Sea. His actions and demeanor settled our nerves about entering this former enemy port. Our bridge watch team and conning officer performed flawlessly and drove THE SULLIVANS smartly starboard side to the pier as planned while a Bulgarian military band played music in honor of our arrival.

The Bulgarian pilot's competence was greatly appreciated. His efforts made the most difficult stage of this visit go smoothly, and inspired our exercise planners to demonstrate an equal level of professionalism for the upcoming inport and at sea events we had come here to execute. The pilot and Bulgarian Navy officials showered our crew with compliments and hospitality. Many of our sailors were impressed and wanted to return this respect and hospitality in kind, volunteering in numbers for several community relations projects at local elementary schools. The lesson learned here was that when just one person does his job well it can make everything go smoother and inspire others to do the same. Unexpected excellence is a wonderful surprise when you do not want to be Magellan.

Community relations projects Varna, Bulgaria 2007

*Children performing traditional Bulgarian folk dance
during crew visit to elementary school*

The port visit and subsequent exercises with the Bulgarian and Romanian navies went exceptionally well. USS THE SULLIVANS (DDG-68) led the efforts to conduct the first trilateral at-sea exercise between the U.S., Bulgarian, and Romanian navies. USS THE SULLIVANS (DDG-68), the Romanian warship REGELE FERDINAND (F-221) and the Bulgarian Navy's Koni class frigate BGS SMELI (FFG-11) operated successfully at sea, conducting division tactics (DIVTACs), underway replenishment practice approaches; communication drills; and visit, board, search, and seizure exercises. This trilateral exercise was beneficial for all partic-ipants and set the standard for future at-sea training with our new NATO partners, Bulgaria and Romania.

The crew of USS THE SULLIVANS (DDG-68) also conducted community relations projects at some local schools, played volleyball against the

Bulgarian Naval Academy's team, and visited the sites in and around Varna. We also hosted the U.S. Ambassador to Bulgaria and held a reception in honor of our hosts. It all went well, and the crew enjoyed visiting Varna. Success in Varna started with our crew doing their homework and the pilot doing his. This caused a positive chain reaction that led to improved NATO maritime capabilities and a sincere strengthening of the partnership between the U.S., Romanian, and Bulgarian navies. We successfully completed our mission in the name of professionalism and friendship.

Our Magellan mission in Varna resulted in success and many lessons learned for our crew as well as the crews of BGS SMELI (FFG-11) and REGELE FERDINAND (F-221). The captains of BGS SMELI and REGELE FERDINAND were not initially jazzed when they learned that all our ships would have to work together and execute tasking that no one had ever done before. The fact is most warship captains that I have met do not want to be Magellan either. Some may seek fame, glory, and riches, but most just want their crews to be well trained and safe when operating at sea. Unexpected excellence is always a welcome gift. Demonstrations of competence and professionalism can also spark a contagious competitive spirit amongst crews.

Not being Magellan did not mean avoiding all risks. Sometimes it is necessary to be the first crew and ship to undertake a mission or visit a new port. What I wanted to convey to our crew about not being Magellan was that we must all do our homework. Being the first to do something was not as important as being prepared, professional, and consistently competent. Perhaps 2,000 years ago in the Mediterranean and Black Seas there might have been a few yet undiscovered ports, but in 2007 there were none. Someone had been Magellan in this part of the world long ago. Meaning that there was plenty of information out there on every port, pier, and harbor we would be tasked to visit. We just had to do our homework and uncover the lessons learned. The bottom line up front was we should never go into any event cold. Magellan did not know what lay out beyond the horizon, but we do. Do the research; do the work first. Magellan took on too much risk and paid the ultimate price. Fame and fortune are not the driving forces behind what USS THE SULLIVANS (DDG-68) and the U.S. Navy do. *We Stick Together* to defend and protect the United States and each other not to be Magellan.

CHAPTER 17

WHO ARE YOUR HEROES?

George Washington - Abraham Lincoln - Jackie Robinson - Jim Plunkett - Antonio Ribeiro

Merriam-Webster's Dictionary defines a hero as "a person who is admired for great or brave acts or fine qualities ... a person who shows great courage."[46] Most people with a grasp of history would probably agree that George Washington, Abraham Lincoln, and Jackie Robinson all fit this definition, but heroes are subjective interpretations in our minds. Our heroes greatly influence us—especially high achievers with exacting standards. People imagine heroes to be better than themselves, a perfect Platonic form of how we should act and who we should strive to be. Learn a person's heroes and you gain a certain insight into their personality and character.

---

46 https://www.merriam-webster.com/dictionary/hero. Definition of "hero" downloaded June 26, 2021.

I believed this to be true back in 2006 when I took command of USS THE SULLIVANS (DDG-68), and still do today. When I was in the Command Leadership School in Newport many years ago, the instructors made the students draft a list of who their heroes were and then present this list to our fellow classmates. We had to stand up and explain why these particular people inspired us. These lists were personal and varied greatly. There were agreements, disagreements, and passionate discussions about who our heroes were. This exercise made the students focus on something many of us never really thought about but spoke volumes about who we were as leaders. I saved my list and referred to it from time to time to remember who my heroes were.

My Roman Catholic upbringing conditioned me to venerate saints but not heroes, especially the mythical, pagan kind. Admittedly I was not well read on famous Greek heroes such as Achilles, Hercules, Odysseus, or Prometheus, but was more familiar with modern superheroes such as Superman, Batman, Wonder Woman, and Aquaman. I always admired George Washington and Abraham Lincoln for their heroic deeds. Leading the American Revolution and keeping the union together were certainly heroic feats in my mind. Later in school I would learn about the hero's journey and how George Lucas used this model to great effect in the epic film *Star Wars*.

In his famous book, *The Hero with a Thousand Faces*, Joseph Campbell describes a hero as someone who "ventures forth from the world of common day into a region of supernatural wonder: fabulous forces are there encountered and a decisive victory is won: the hero comes back from this mysterious adventure with the power to bestow boons on his fellow man."[47] This formula works well in literature, myth, and movies but not always in real life.

I think heroes—real heroes—are those individuals that influenced us the most as we became adults. When I was a boy, I idolized sports figures mostly. Jackie Robinson and Jim Plunkett were my biggest heroes. I remember holding a Jackie Robinson baseball card in my hands. I wish I would have held on to that card today. His batting average, home runs, and stolen base statistics were impressive, but his journey to the big leagues was what hooked me. Jackie Robinson overcame tremendous cultural hurdles and racism while maintaining his character. He was an exceptional athlete but an even better role model.

Jim Plunkett was an NFL quarterback in the 1970s and 1980s. When he played for the New England Patriots, I would watch him on TV and at Schaefer Stadium (known today as Gillette Stadium) in Foxboro, MA. Jim Plunkett was born in San Jose, CA, to a poor Mexican-American family, and both his parents were blind. He wore the number 16 and went on to win two Superbowl championships with the Oakland Raiders. He played hard and never gave up. I remember reading about his hero's journey from a book on NFL stars that I got at a school book mobile. Both Jackie Robinson and Jim Plunkett inspired me and were my heroes. Overcoming obstacles, pursuing their passion, and maintaining their character were traits I wanted to emulate.

Another big hero and influencer in my life was my grandfather Antonio Ribeiro. He was a hard working man who immigrated to the United States in 1944. He spoke little English but was kind and patient, especially with

---

47 Joseph Campbell, The Hero with a Thousand Faces, Pantheon Books, 1949, downloaded quote from https://en.wikipedia.org/wiki/The_Hero_with_a_Thousand_Faces on June 26, 2021.

me. He fished from dories on the Grand Banks with the Portuguese fishing fleet in the 1930s. His sea stories and selfless demeanor encouraged me to go to sea. I tried hard to model my character after his. He passed away in 1991, but his influence on me lives on. I think about him and my list of heroes often, especially when I need to regain focus on what is most important in life.

Whether it is religious figures, presidents, athletes, or grandfathers, everyone has heroes they admire. Learning the heroes of our sailors greatly aided in connecting and inspiring them to do good. And if some sailors were not sure who their heroes were, USS THE SULLIVANS (DDG-68) had five brothers who could fit the bill.

USS THE SULLIVANS (DDG-68) belt buckle circa 2006

George, Francis, Joseph, Madison, and Albert Sullivan were heroes for doing their part and sticking together. They did not ask to be heroes, nor would they likely admit to being heroic if they had the chance. Heroes are selfless and sacrifice for others. The New Testament tells us, "No one has greater love than this, to lay down one's life for one's friends."[48] The Sullivan brothers joined the Navy after losing a friend in the attack on Pearl Harbor and then laid down their lives for all Americans. They exceeded the standard. Their example is truly inspiring; the Sullivans were real heroes. Their heroism continues to inspire Americans today, especially those with a connection to DD-537 or DDG-68.

There are some philosophers, such as Ayn Rand, author of *Atlas Shrugged* and *The Fountainhead*, that claim that altruism and selflessness are stupid and even evil. Ayn Rand believed that the altruistic and selfless tendencies of men were manipulated by organized religion and totalitarian states to take away people's individual rights. She had firsthand evidence of this as she was born and raised in the Soviet Union. Ayn Rand probably did not have many heroes outside of rational philosophers such as Aristotle and her fictional character John Galt. Ayn Rand's fictionalized hero was a great philosopher and inventor, who she believed drove society forward. Ayn Rand did not have any heroes who were selfless or sacrificed themselves for the betterment of others.

Because heroes represent an individual's deep beliefs and personal values, people's heroes can be a very sensitive subject area. Tread lightly when you discuss a person's heroes. A reflexive facial expression or raised eyebrow when a friend, colleague, or sailor mentions their favorite hero could be construed as fighting words by some. Critiquing someone else's heros accidently or overtly is a sure recipe for heated debate and even fisticuffs. This is because a person's deepest beliefs, values, and dreams are connected to their heroes. Disrespect or demean a

---

48 John 15:13, The New American Bible, World Catholic Press, Printed in Canada, 1987, p.1160.

person's heroes, and you may be guilty of disrespecting and demeaning them as human beings.

Who are your heroes? Do you keep a written list? What values and character traits do you try and emulate? These are questions we should all think about from time to time. My list of heroes keeps growing and growing. The Sullivan brothers became part of my list in 2005. Their sacrifice is something I think about quite often. There are many heroes who walk among us. Most of them do not want to be known. Selflessness is like that.

CHAPTER 18

THE POWER OF SELFLESS LEADERSHIP

12/25/06 1:15 am

USS THE SULLIVANS (DDG-68) anchored in Gaeta, Italy December 25, 2006

Abraham Lincoln once famously said, "a house divided against itself cannot stand." He took this quote from the Bible because it was simple and had the moral impact he wanted to convey. It also meshed nicely with America's motto of *E Pluribus Unum*—out of many one. Some say the moral conviction Lincoln expressed in this one quote was the reason he was elected President. Selfless moral conviction for a cause, company, or one's colleagues can be harnessed to make any organization great. Selflessness is a trait people cherish but do not always practice themselves. Putting the needs and desires of others consistently above your own is a rare quality in political leaders, although it should not be.

When a leader naturally and honestly conveys his or her conviction for a cause, and pursues it every day selflessly, people will naturally follow. Most people want to belong to something bigger than themselves. They will sacrifice and work harder to contribute to help a cause they believe in, especially if they think it can win. Everyone yearns to be on a winning team. Some individuals will use a good cause or a winning team to pursue their own self interests. "Band-wagoning" is also a natural phenomenon because most people seek the safety of the herd, the security of the winning team. Good leaders understand these traits intuitively and can harness them for the greater good. Leaders who are selfless and have strong emotional intelligence are adept at understanding a person's true character. Strong moral conviction is hard to fake, especially under the scrutiny of those who are selfless themselves, like most sailors that volunteer to serve in the U.S. Navy.

This might sound like a religious sermon or philosophical mumbo-jumbo, but it is truth. Human beings have evolved and/or been designed to seek the truth. Character counts and is the only thing we take beyond the grave. We want our leaders to be righteous, good people. We expect them to win and make our lives better, all the while setting the example and not falling short morally, even if we do ourselves. The good king, the great president, the victorious general, these are all archetypes of leaders we wish we could have. This is a lot to ask of flawed, error-prone humans. Often when someone is a strong leader with clear moral convictions, he or she is scrutinized and attacked by the very people they are trying to show what right looks like. Moses, Jesus, Joan of Arc, and Abraham Lincoln fit this description in my mind. They were all selfless leaders who were willing to sacrifice their personal desires and even themselves for others. They also all had the courage of their convictions and led by personal example; do as I do not do as I say.

Selfless individuals, unfortunately, do not naturally rise-up to lead good causes or organizations. Cliches such as "only the good die young" and "nice guys finish last" are based on truth. The natural tendency of all bureaucracy is to punish those who make work or promote change. Unfortunately, more often than not, ambitious people, who are prideful and ruthless, rise to power in pursuit of glory and self-interest. This is the natural state of things in this world. It is neither right nor wrong; it just is—and it should be the fundamental truth upon which all organizational hierarchies are structured. This includes the U.S. Navy.

So how should we structure organizations so that the selfless, humble, and competent become the leaders? How do we prevent the nice guy who can win from finishing last? That is the challenge for all government bureaucracies and military organizations. Entities that reward merit, talent, and conviction over nepotism, cronyism, and vanity tend to achieve long-term success. Talented, selfless people are attracted to other talented, selfless people, which causes collective virtue to grow and better outcomes for all. Any organization that can structure itself so that its core values drive the incubation and promotion of future leaders who are selfless, humble, and competent will be on the road to self-sustaining success. For over 29 years I have had faith that this is how the U.S. Navy operates. It promotes the best and brightest among us, most of whom are selfless, caring individuals, who in turn, promote the same values going forward. This self-sustaining cycle is what has made the

U.S. Navy the strongest maritime force in history in terms of firepower and character.

USS THE SULLIVANS (DDG-68) was commissioned into service April 19, 1997. She was blessed with selfless, talented leadership, a great crew, and a passionate sponsor from her first days of service. The ship performed well and earned a great waterfront reputation over time. And while morale sometimes dipped and things went wrong, new crews and new leadership could always fall back on the selfless example of the Sullivan brothers and the motto of *We Stick Together*. These three simple words provided the moral conviction to focus on teamwork, the mission, and the pursuit of excellence. It was simple, sincere, and powerful, and it worked.

Strong moral conviction and humility are not traits of the fainthearted. Strength and power arise from selfless moral conviction. Good leaders know how to blend strong moral conviction with a competitive spirit. Winning does not have to weaken one's humility or selflessness, but it does present new challenges and temptations. Anyone who has been a leader understands that it is much harder to keep a winning organization on top then lead an under-performing one out of the cellar.

What is the definition of "good leadership"? There are thousands of books on the subject and so many self-proclaimed experts out there that it may seem difficult to know where to begin a focused study of the subject. For me good leadership boils down to this: inspiring people to work towards a common goal for the greater good.

Leadership is different than management. Management is about programs and things. I don't know any person that yearns to be managed, but most of us do want to be led. Simply put, leadership is not about bossing people around; it is the art of getting people to do great things because they want to.

I consider myself very fortunate to have had the opportunity to lead men and women ashore and at sea for more than 29 years in the U.S. Navy. I commanded two ships and three shore-based organizations. I learned and adapted all along the way. In the military if you like to lead you will be given the opportunity to do so over and over again.

My first real experience as a leader came when I was 18 years old and a sophomore at Norwich University, the Military College of Vermont. I volunteered for a leadership position as a squad leader for incoming freshmen. My job was to look after and train a squad of ten new recruits in basic military instruction and help them become Norwich cadets and successful undergraduate students. It was hard work and very challenging, but from that day forward I decided that leading people was what I wanted to do with my life, and the Navy has continually given me many challenging opportunities to do so.

Since those early days in college all the way up to the challenge of commanding U.S. Navy warships at sea, what I discovered was that good leadership is really all about one's own character. When I use the word "character," I am referring to an individual's personal qualities, virtues and behavior—basically how a person treats other people. In the Navy you spend 17 to 19 years on average observing, training, and learning how to be a leader before you can earn the privilege of being selected to be a captain and are allowed to lead sailors at sea by yourself.

I have been a fan of NFL football ever since I can remember. I enjoyed playing football and respected all the athletes who made it to the pros. It is a difficult eight-year journey on average for those fortunate few driven and talented athletes who perform at the highest level from high school through college and earn a shot to play one season in the NFL. The path to commanding a U.S. Navy warship is an even more arduous journey. Commanding a U.S. Navy warship takes eight years of high school and college, plus another 15 to 18 years of service for your first shot at command. In 2015 there were approximately 1,700 players in the National Football League, and only 275 U.S. Navy ships to command. That means that there are almost six times as many NFL professional athletes as there are men and women commanding U.S. Navy ships. The average NFL salary is around one million dollars a year. A Navy warship commander is lucky if he or she earns one-tenth of that amount. So if one's goal in life is making money, do not choose leadership positions in the U.S. Navy. Even the most senior admiral in the U.S. Navy will never earn close to what an average NFL player makes.

The truth is leadership is not about money; it is about something much more important. Leaders who are passionate about making peoples' lives, businesses, or organizations better stand out from the rest. Passion not money is the currency of leadership. Leaders earn their true reward and satisfaction by seeing their people succeed. Good leaders, by definition, achieve positive results and accomplish the mission. Great leaders are those that do this and maintain their character.

Good leadership is connected directly to good training and education, especially in the armed forces. For those who truly want to be good leaders, it is necessary to get down in the trenches with the people you are charged with leading, and understand what it is you are asking them to do from their vantage point. If you were in their shoes instead of yours, what would it take for you to do the job? Would you yourself be willing to do it? If the answer is no, then you might want to rethink why you are trying to get others to do said task.

Leadership is not easy and can be very hard work, but it is necessary to achieve great results. Someone has to take charge and organize the group, team, or squad to achieve the objective. In short, a leader should always try and set the example for others to follow. There is no app for this or quick down-load you can pull off the internet. As a leader you have to be ready and willing to roll up your sleeves and put in the extra hours to ensure a task, mission, or plan is completed and successful. Great leaders naturally set the example for others to follow.

When you assume a leadership position, whether in school, in business, or in public service, people will always expect more from you. People want their leaders to be morally and ethically better than they are them-selves. This is why so many of us are often disappointed when we find out our leaders have fallen short of our expectations. This may not seem fair or right, but it is the burden that comes with leadership.

Good leadership starts with your own character. Everyone is capable of strengthening their character, and can make the choice not to lie, cheat, or steal, and always do the right thing even when no one is watching. In reality, short-term successes can be gained by running roughshod over people and working them harder and harder. I have seen this style of leadership in action and suffered under it. As soon as this type of leader leaves the room, however, most positive work stops. Fear and intimi-dation can be effective in the short term, but over time these qualities bring bad results and long-term pain. This is my personal experience and professional opinion.

Leaders have to make tough decisions all the time. Many times these decisions will make people angry. Leadership is not a popularity contest, and doing what is right for the mission, objective, or team is not always going to be easy or welcomed by those you are chosen to lead. All you can do is tell your people the truth and show them the way ahead. If you have their trust and confidence, they will follow you through to the end, even though they may not agree with some of the methods or decisions that you chose along the way.

Another key element of leadership is humility. Leadership should not be about the perks that come with a position, or putting your own personal interests ahead of those you are charged with leading. The mission, objective, or team should always be the clear goal. If you put your people first, and show them that you do not lie, cheat, or steal nor tolerate those who do, they will have trust in you, and trust is the foundation for great leadership. It really is that simple.

We all expect our leaders to succeed. Often times when you are in a leadership position, unfortunately, you make decisions that lead to failure. I believe it is a universal law that all leaders will have failures at one time or another. A key aspect of great leadership is learning from these failures. Great leaders fail but this is not often highlighted or documented in the history books. What is noted is that great leaders throughout history seem to develop the ability to overcome adversity, remain positive even in the worst times, and rally their people again, and again until the goal is successfully achieved. Great leaders do not make the same mistakes twice and take a deep interest in lessons learned. Great leaders also have determination and stamina towards clearly articulated goals. Successful leaders are able to provide a vision of where they want to take an organization or group and empower their people to do what is needed to achieve it.

John Quincy Adams, a famous American statesman, and the sixth president of the United States, said, "If your actions inspire others to dream more, learn more, do more and become more, you are a leader."

Steve Jobs, the former cofounder and CEO of Apple, thought that leadership was about innovation. He said, "Innovation distinguishes between a leader and a follower."

Nelson Mandela, the first Black president of South Africa, believed, "It is better to lead from behind and to put others in front, especially when you celebrate victory when nice things occur; you take the front line when there is danger. Then people will appreciate your leadership."

Martin Luther King, Jr., the great American civil rights leader and activist, said, "A leader is not a searcher for consensus but a molder of consensus."

Colin Powell, a retired four-star general and former secretary of state, once said "Leadership is solving problems. The day soldiers stop bringing you their problems is the day you have stopped leading them."

And finally, the Supreme Allied Commander during World War II, and later the 34th President of the United States, Dwight D. Eisenhower believed,

"Leadership is the art of getting someone else to do something you want done because he wants to do it."[49]

---

49 The quotes from John Quincy Adams, Nelson Mandela, Steve Jobs, General Eisenhower, and Colin Powell were verified in 2014 for a speech given to the American Overseas School of Rome on leadership by Capt Tony Parisi, USN, the Senior Defense Official and Defense Attaché to Italy.

For me when I think about these powerful and meaningful quotes on leadership, it all boils down to character, setting the example and truly understanding the people you are leading. The secret to great leadership is simple: it is nothing more than providing people a vision and then empowering them to achieve it.

All the leaders quoted above achieved incredible results and made history because they were able to motivate other human beings to sacrifice and work together towards a common goal. It is important to remember that it is the people that we lead who get things done and bring about success. Sometimes leaders believe that they are somehow special or privileged because of the results their people achieve. This is a false notion caused by hubris and vanity. The ancients warned us all that "pride comes before a fall." All leaders should heed this warning or at least empower those they trust to look them in the eye and repeat these words of wisdom slowly until they are understood. If you start to believe that you are a great leader and that you have magical abilities or were chosen to lead, that should be a red flag that you are on the road to dismal failure as history has proven over and over again.

In the U.S. Navy, you are taught that in order to be a great leader you must first be a good follower. When you are forced to be a follower you clearly understand what qualities you want in your leader. I found that I wanted a leader that did not lie, cheat, or steal nor tolerated those who did. I wanted my leaders to be fair and humble, but also strong and determined. As a follower I wanted to trust my leader.

Becoming a leader starts with analyzing what kind of person you are and want to become. If you want to be a great leader you first must focus on yourself and strengthening your character. You must treat the people you lead with respect and set the standard for them to follow. Leadership is very hard work and that is why most people do not choose to be leaders. The real reward of leadership follows from the satisfaction of helping people achieve things they never thought they could do on their own. It is the smile that comes across your face when you inspire your team, business, or ship to strive for excellence in your absence. Leadership is not about personal gain or advancing one's career, but accomplishing the mission and helping people succeed.

So what practical advice do the paragraphs above offer? What are the lessons learned here? Strong moral conviction is a powerful leadership tool. It must be sincere and consistent. Selflessness can be its own reward and will inspire others to act, sacrifice, and exceed the standards. Organizations should promote their best people based on performance, ability, and above all character. The U.S. Navy was created, continually improved, and succesful in war because of great leaders and the sailors they led. Becoming a leader in the U.S. Navy, or anywhere, means first understanding one's own character.

The U.S. Navy wisely provides commanding officers the opportunity to promote hard working, potential leaders from within. Sometimes sailors are trapped in rating groups that have small promotion quotas or they just do not test well on standardized advancement exams. Other sailors might have a minor disciplinary infraction in their records that prevents their natural advancement to the next paygrade. For these reasons and many more commanding officers at sea are given the authority to choose some of the Navy's next generation of leaders locally. This program was called the Command Advancement Program (CAP).[50]

---

50 The program name has changed since 2007. It is now known as MAP, or the Meritorious Advancement Program.

Enlisted sailors in the U.S. Navy move up in pay grade and rank based on time in service, Navy-wide advancement exams, and a point system based on their performance. The system works well most of the time, but there is an expression amongst sailors: "choose your rate; choose your fate." Sometimes certain rates, such as sonar technician (STG) or machinery repairman (MR) might be more difficult to advance in than other rates. This can be due to retention, previous promotions, quotas, and other variables governed by the U.S. Navy's Bureau of Personnel (BUPERS).

In USS THE SULLIVANS (DDG-68) we reserved the Command Advancement Program to promote those sailors who demonstrated selflessness, worked hard, and were ready for new leadership positions. The chief's mess would vet the candidates. Names would be proposed to the commanding officer up the chain of command and then the right individuals selected. Commanding officers only had a few quotas per year to use in this program, so selections were difficult, especially since USS THE SULLIVANS (DDG-68) had an abundance of selfless self-start-ing sailors.

Commanding Officer's call USS THE SULLIVANS (DDG-68) at sea in 2006

USS THE SULLIVANS (DDG-68) award ceremony at sea in 2007

The CAP was an opportunity to reward selflessness and sailors of strong character for their efforts. We would make the announcement during a planned award ceremony as a surprise. Sailors would be called forward and then told they were being promoted. The crew would cheer and clap and the Sailor being advanced would be surprised and sometimes teary eyed. Good things do happen to good people. The Command Advancement Program was just one venue where selflessness was rewarded and appreciated.

Admiral Arleigh Burke, USN (1901-1996)

"Leadership is understanding people and involving them to help you do a job. That takes all of the good characteristics, like integrity, dedication

of purpose, selflessness, knowledge, skill, implacability, as well as deter-mination not to accept failure."[51] Admiral Arleigh Burke

Great U.S. Navy leaders like Admiral Arleigh Burke understood the power of selfless leadership. Many of us in the Navy tried our best to follow his example. I know this was the case during my time in USS THE SULLIVANS (DDG-68) because I saw it happen at all levels, from E-3 to O-5. Our ballcaps, T-shirts, belt buckles, coins, and ship were emblazoned with *We Stick Together.* Everyone in the crew understood that these simple words called us to be selfless and sacrifice for our shipmates in time of need. *We Stick Together* was not a gimmick or propaganda but an example of how we should all act towards one another. We took it seriously and it meant something to us then and now.

---

51 https://www.inspiringquotes.us/author/6913-arleigh-burke. Downloaded June 27, 2021.

CHAPTER 19:

FORGIVE US OUR TRESPASSES
AS WE FORGIVE THOSE WHO
TRESPASS AGAINST US

James Tissot's The Lord's Prayer Brooklyn Museum

The most important lessons we learn come during our youth and get repeated over and over the rest of our life. Catholic school and religious education were mandatory in my family. I attended the St. Mel's Day School and Our Lady of Good Voyage Roman Catholic church in Gloucester. I wore uniforms most of my life. From first through fourth grade, I wore blue trousers, hard-toed dark shoes, and a light blue button-down shirt with a black tie. Later the nuns would ease the dress code a bit and permit us the opportunity to wear a white turtle-neck, long-sleeve shirt under a blue V-neck sweater. In military college I wore army greens, and in the Navy, working khakis. The Roman Catholic Church, the Military College of Vermont, and the U.S. Navy were all historic institutions that survived the test of time by holding to certain values across generations. They were strict and firm, but fair if you followed the rules. Many of the lessons learned in these institutions overlapped and reinforced one another.

One of the first real lessons I remember learning in life was memorizing the Our Father (*Pater Noster* in Latin) and having to repeat it back aloud. Catholic nuns in habits and priests would quiz us on this in and out of the classroom. After receiving the sacrament of penance (aka confession) in second grade, the Our Father, along with the Hail Mary, were required knowledge for your act of contrition. You would confess your sins to the priest in the confessional and receive a certain number of Our Fathers and Hail Marys to recite to yourself while kneeling at the altar. The priest would watch you out of the corner of his eye even while hearing someone else's confession. You had better kneel for the allotted amount of time it took to say six Our Fathers and ten Hail Marys, or you would be questioned as to why you were departing so fast. Learning to do verbatim repeat backs came early in life to young Roman Catholics. It was not a surprise when I learned this was also required for U.S. Navy sailors.

When a sailor receives a formal order on watch, they are required to repeat it back to show they received it, understood it, and plan to carry it out. If the order was given in error, the verbatim repeat back served as feedback (i.e., questioning attitude) to the issuer.

Our Lady of Good Voyage Roman Catholic church in Gloucester, MA

The former St. Mel's Day School, Gloucester, MA–It officially closed in 1992

Having too much of a questioning attitude in Catholic school, however, was not something that was promoted, especially when questioning any core lesson or prayer. I always wanted to know why the Our Father was so special but did not dare ask. Wooden rulers across your knuckles and phone calls home to parents were the nuns' pre-planned responses for insubordinate children. We did not salute the nuns in Catholic school, but we did obey. I was curious but remained quiet, at least regarding this question. For those who have forgotten or perhaps were never exposed to the Our Father in English, here it is:

The Lord's Prayer (aka Our Father)

Our Father who art in Heaven
Hallowed be thy name.
Thy kingdom come, thy will be done,
on earth as it is in Heaven.
Give us this day our daily bread
and forgive us our trespasses, as we forgive those who trespass
against us.
Lead us not into temptation
but deliver us from evil.
For thine is the kingdom and the power and the glory, forever.
Amen

Pretty simple, right? But what do the words really mean? Is this an order, an administrative request, or merely a suggestion? That is a lot to unpack, so I will just focus on the second clause of the third sentence. "Forgive us our trespasses as we forgive those who trespass against us." This phrase really made me think, and still does. As a boy, I thought trespass meant to walk across someone else's property or lawn when they did not want you to. I was not sure where God's lawn was, and I was okay with forgiving those who came across ours if they were just passing through. I could not see the big deal here.

Later I learned the Lord's Prayer, or the Our Father, was Jesus's response to His disciples when asked how they should pray. In U.S. Navy terminology, the disciples were not yet PQS (Personal Qualification Standard) qualified and needed instruction. Jesus was the subject matter expert and provided them the Our Father, which was like Engineering Operating Casualty Control (EOCC) procedures to manage one's soul. You had to memorize and do the immediate actions, and then go back and read the words to make sure you did not miss a step. This made sense. This is what we teach all U.S. Navy sailors to do because it works to prevent major catastrophes from happening at sea.

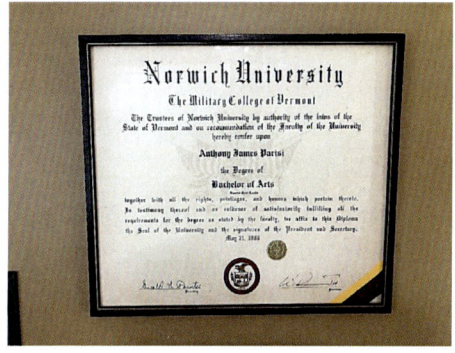

Capt Tony Parisi's Norwich diploma from 1988

Norwich cadet handbook (aka rook book)

I learned a similar message when I was a cadet at Norwich University, the Military College of Vermont. We had to learn the Cadet's Creed and pledge to "not lie, cheat or steal, nor tolerate those who do." Norwich's motto was "Essayons," which was translated from French to mean "I will try." I took these words to heart and always tried my best to live by them. The overlapping values of my church, my college, and my Navy guided me when in command of USS THE SULLIVANS (DDG-68). These values helped forge my character and were reenforced by the ship's motto, *We Stick Together*. It all made perfect sense to me and provided a strong moral foundation that served as the keel of our command philosophy.

I also learned that the word "trespass" in the Our Father was translated from Latin, where its original meaning referred to debts or sins. I knew things could easily be lost in translation, as I grew up in a bilingual household. Miscommunication and not listening thoroughly were common problems in the Navy. Words can have different meanings if they are used in the wrong context. I now could see the line "forgive us our trespasses as we forgive those who trespass against us" meant to forgive people for their acts against you, as God does for us all. As I grew older and wiser, I would learn that forgiveness does not mean forgetting what people did to you or those you love. It means letting go of the anger and resentment that builds up inside you when you realize you have been wronged. It also means treat others as you expect to be treated.

USS THE SULLIVANS (DDG-68) commissioning poster 1997

Waterloo Daily Courier from January 19, 1943

The Sullivan brothers' ancestors immigrated to the United States from Ireland in the late 1840s during the great potato famine. George, Francis, Joseph, Madison, and Albert were raised as Roman Catholics during the Great Depression. They were rich in spirit and family pride. Like many of us, they probably went to church because their mother made them. I am sure they had similar lessons about the Our Father and Hail Mary during their catechism studies. Perhaps they were drawn to the line "Give us this day our daily bread …" as that was their struggle at the time. Had they lived, perhaps they too would have relearned the lessons in the Lord's Prayer and realized that the Church and U.S. Navy shared the same values: honor, courage, and commitment.

The structures of the Roman Catholic Church and the U.S. Navy are similar in many ways. There are regulations, a chain of command, uniforms, and bases of operations (aka archdiocese in Catholic parlance). Both institutions promote selfless service to a cause greater than self and require sacrifice. Crews and congregations are captive audiences that rely on guidance and direction from the pulpit. Both the Church and Navy have qualification standards that must be completed and witnessed by other members. There are classes, tests, and protocols that are expected to be followed. The values of the Church and the Navy overlap in many areas, with the Golden Rule "do unto others as you would have them do unto you" essential to both. The similarities go on and on, which might explain why so many Catholics, like the Sullivans, chose to serve in the U.S. Navy.

Religion and spirituality are very personal matters. The U.S. Navy does not have a preferred religion or faith for sailors and neither did USS THE SULLIVANS. Although I consider myself Christian, I also studied many other faiths and spiritual practices, learning insights and lessons from them all. USS THE SULLIVANS (DDG-68) had Sailors from every religion and denomination. *We Stick Together* was a universal concept that everyone could relate to and understand. It was not bound by cannon law or dogma, but by a shared mental model that all our crew understood.

In USS THE SULLIVANS (DDG-68), and all U.S. Navy ships that I have had the privilege of serving in, the Golden Rule was the entering argument and always in effect. When sailors trespassed against their shipmates, justice was supposed to be swift and severe, like a wooden ruler across your knuckles. The Church and the Navy are not perfect institutions, they are inherently flawed because they are built and managed by people. When they screw up, they need to be held accountable. People make mistakes. The Our Father and SSOPP help mitigate human error when followed. We should forgive those who violate both but also hold them accountable for their actions and inactions. This is what I realized while in command of USS THE SULLIVANS (DDG-68).

I also came to realize that "forgive us our trespasses as we forgive those who trespass against us" was directive in nature, applied to all people all the time, and requires constant attention to be effective. When you forgive you should not forget but release your animosity and anger and move on. Accountability and forgiveness are not inversely proportional. Sailors can and should do both. As former President John F. Kennedy, an Irish-Catholic, U.S. Navy surface warfare officer in World War II, once said, "Forgive our enemies, but never forget their names."[52]

---

52 https://www.brainyquote.com/quotes/john_f_kennedy_103659#:~:text=Forgive%20your%20enemies%2C%20but%20never%20forget%20their%20names. Downloaded June 28, 2021.

CHAPTER 20

IT ALL DEPENDS ON HOW YOU FRAME IT

A country road in an open picture frame … its true meaning and beauty depend on how you frame it.

"It all depends on how we look at things, and not on how things are in themselves. The least of things with a meaning is worth more in life than the greatest of things without it."[53]

Carl Gustav Jung

---

53 https://www.goodreads.com/quotes/55469-it-all-depends-on-how-we-look-at-things-and. Quote by Carl Gustav Jung downloaded October 1, 2021.

CDR Tony Parisi addressing crew via 1MC 2006

The Bosun's pipe trills and the 1MC (ship's announcement system) hand-set is passed to the captain on the bridge. The black button that turns on the microphone is already depressed, which means there will be about 5 to 10 seconds for me to capture the crew's attention and let them know what is going on. If I say something that goes against their expectations, I may get their rapt attention but also immediately reduce morale and distract them from the mission. Moods are contagious aboard ship. The tone and delivery of the message matters. If I start to ramble and ad lib, the command master chief and executive officer move closer and begin to gesticulate. It all depends on how I frame it.

In USS THE SULLIVANS (DDG-68) we tried to keep the crew well informed, especially underway. That meant a no-notice 1MC announce-ment from the commanding officer about the schedule changing or some event that shifted our priorities every couple of days. Occasionally the executive officer, command master chief, or department head would take to the inner airwaves and let the crew know what was happening. Our leadership triad, the executive officer (XO), command master chief (CMC), and I would normally meet prior to anyone of us taking to the 1MC. We all agreed that a unified well-thought out and sincere message was the best form of information delivery to the 300-plus souls aboard USS THE SULLIVANS (DDG-68). They deserved and needed to hear the truth, especially when we were at sea and far from home.

There is a lot of psychology and research behind getting people's attention. There are many theories and concepts rooted in biology and science, like expectancy violation theory, which predicts that people will pay more attention when their expectations are not met or exceeded. There is also the concept of directed deference, which hypothesizes that people's thinking and brains slow and shut down when they believe an expert is giving advice. There is the Zeigarnik effect, which postulates that our memories are purposefully tuned to remember fragments and incomplete stories. All this could be true, but I was not aware of any of these theories when I was in command. I believed that our crew wanted sincerity, respect, and a fair playing field. Our leadership triad never sugar-coated bad news or overhyped the good. We did not have time, and we were bad liars. That is how we framed it.

On our Mediterranean and Black Seas deployment, every USS THE SULLIVANS (DDG-68) sailor would be an ambassador and spokesman of our Navy, nation, and ship. They needed the facts and the latest information because that was the basis of our mission. In the post-Cold War, post-9/11 world, this is true for all U.S. Navy sailors going ashore overseas on liberty while deployed. The stereotype of the drunken sailor with lots of cash to spend has long since passed. In 2006 and 2007, in the Sixth Fleet area of operations, there was a strict dress code and specific rules of behavior that had to be followed for all sailors going ashore. Our mission was to engage with the host nation's military and improve relations. Liberty was authorized, but most of our time in port was spent working with foreign militaries, planning exercises, and hosting meetings. While this was hard work, it could also be fun. It all depended on how we framed it.

Israeli VBSS Exercise aboard USS THE SULLIVANS (DDG-68) March 2007

*VIP reception for Israeli military and civilian officials
in port Haifa, Israel March 2007*

When THE SULLIVANS arrived overseas in a port, local and U.S. embassy team representatives would normally come aboard and explain the rules and any specific cultural oddities that our crew might need to be familiar with. They would also put out the off-limits areas as well as the best places for our crew to go. This information would then be passed on to the crew as part of a liberty brief.

The liberty brief is a common occurrence in the U.S. Navy. It is required and covers the rules, overnight policy, safety, and security protocols everyone must follow. How the information is delivered and presented to the individual sailor matters. If a division officer or chief puts out the information with negative tones and disparaging comments, then the sailors will be influenced negatively, might not go ashore much, and might not enjoy the port. In USS THE SULLIVANS (DDG-68), we encouraged sailors to take the officially sanctioned and vetted united services organizations (USO) and U.S. Navy morale, welfare, and recreation (MWR) tours. Our leadership triad had been on many of these trips throughout their careers and set the example by using these services in the ports they were offered. Our port visit to Haifa, Israel, was a perfect example of this and would prove to be one of the most memorable visits of my 29-year Navy career.

USS THE SULLIVANS (DDG-68) was the first U.S. Navy ship to pull into Haifa following the 2006 Israeli Lebanon War. This violent conflict took place between Israel and the Hezbollah militant group in July 2006, after a raid on Israeli territory resulted in several Israeli soldiers being killed and some taken captive. Israeli military forces retaliated with airstrikes and artillery barrages into Southern Lebanon. Israeli troops then occupied Southern Lebanon and blockaded the area from the sea. On August, 11 2006, the <u>United Nations Security Council</u> unanimously approved <u>United Nations Security Council Resolution 1701</u> (UNSCR 1701) to end the hostilities. The Lebanese Army began deploying in Southern Lebanon on August 17, 2006, and the blockade was lifted on September 8, 2006.[54] By October 1, 2006, most Israeli troops had withdrawn from Lebanon and the major battles had ended. Hezbollah's attack on INS HANIT occurred on July 14, 2006. HANIT was homeported in Haifa. USS THE SULLIVANS (DDG-68) arrived in Haifa on March 20, 2007, about six months after the war had officially ended.

---

54 https://en.wikipedia.org/wiki/2006_Lebanon_War#cite. Paraphrased from Wikipedia June 30, 2021. Most of the information here appears to come from BBC reporting.

Political tensions remained high and security was tight in Haifa when we arrived. The rules regarding liberty for our sailors were restricted, so USO- and MWR-sanctioned tours with armed escorts were the best option for those that wanted to see the sights. Our command triad, wardroom, chief's mess, and most of the crew opted for these tours. There were tours to the Dead Sea, Jerusalem, Nazareth, Capernaum, and other historic places. Most of the crew chose the day-long USO-organized trip to Jerusalem and Capernaum, which offered a historical tour of where Jesus had lived, walked, and preached. I chose this tour as well as I remembered doing a similar one many years ago when I was deployed in 1989 and stopped in Haifa with USS FORRESTAL (CV-59).

Our tour guide was a former Israeli Defense Force (IDF) soldier named Joshua (not his real name). Joshua was in his late 40s or early 50s. He had fought in Lebanon in the 1980s and been wounded. He carried an old leatherbound King James Bible and began the tour by telling us that he had converted to Christianity during the war after being wounded and finding the Bible next to him in the dirt. Our tour group listened and many, including me, thought Joshua might be embellishing a bit. His tone sounded sincere, but the story seemed unbelievable. As the tour progressed, many of us started to believe Joshua's conversion and sentiment were truly genuine. Joshua warned us that he called this tour the "F-bombs for Jesus" tour. He explained that his stories and explanations of history would be salty and that he sometimes peppered his English with profanity, as English was not his native language.

The tour began with a bus ride from Haifa to the outskirts of Jerusalem. During this 150-mile bus ride, Joshua set the tone and framed what we would see. He explained that ancient and modern Israel are not the United States, and that we would have to think much smaller scale.

The cities, rivers, and roads we were used to seeing in America dwarf anything that existed in ancient Israel. For our sailors, many of whom had never travelled outside the U.S. before, this came as a shock. They pictured the Jordan River in their minds as being much larger, like the Mississippi or St. John's River, and were floored when they saw that it was no more than a stream or brook.

One of our first stops was the Church of Beatitudes near Capernaum. This church was built near the spot where Jesus preached the sermon on the mount and the miracle of the loaves and fishes was claimed to have happened. As we exited the bus and entered the church, Joshua took me aside and asked if there was anyone in our crew who could sing and sing well. USS THE SULLIVANS (DDG-68) had its own rock band, I explained, and we had lots of crew members who were musically inclined. I pointed to a female sailor that I knew could sing, as I had heard her before when our band, Keelhauled, did a karaoke night on our mess decks. Joshua made note and went on with the tour. Once inside, Joshua gathered the group up, battered leatherbound Bible in hand, and explained that the Church of the Beatitudes was first constructed in the Byzantine era (fourth century AD) to commemorate Jesus's sermon on the mount. In the church was a large plaque in English with the words of the sermon. As we read the words, Joshua walked over to the sailor I had pointed out and then they walked together to the center of the church under the dome. Then in a loud, clear voice she began to sing "Amazing Grace." Her voice was beautiful and the acoustics in the church caused her words to reverberate and echo throughout the structure. Our crew all stopped and stared, as did all the other tourist groups there visiting. Hundreds of tourists and our sailors stopped talking and stood still. We all just listened: "Amazing grace, how sweet the sound, that saved a wretch; like me. I once was lost, but now am found ..."

Church of Beatitudes, near Capernaum, Israel circa 2007

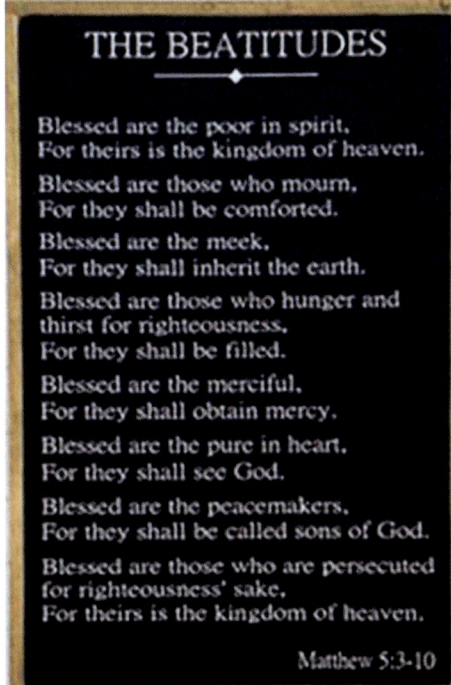

Sermon on the Mount text

Our singing sailor's lyrics hit their targets hard in their hearts and minds. She was singing a cappella but it sounded like she was accompanied by soft melodic music, which carried throughout the large church. Her singing coincided with many sailors reading the Beatitudes, which produced a synchronized rush of spiritual energy for many of us. Tears formed in eyes and some sailors began to weep with joy, while others stood stunned, thinking and wondering what was happening. Joshua caught many off guard, and it had worked. I did not know that our sailor knew the words to "Amazing Grace" or could sing it, but it happened as if planned. Believers and non-believers alike were moved.

After our sailor finished the short hymn, Joshua led us all outside to a hill. He positioned us above him on the hill and opened his Bible and began to read in a soft voice. He read the Beatitudes and then explained it was from near this spot that Jesus had preached the sermon on the mount. Joshua told us to imagine thousands of people listening to his words and then having a meal. That is when the miracle of the loaves and fishes took place. No one supposedly brought food when Jesus spoke here almost 2,000 years ago, but somehow it materialized and was shared amongst the crowd, and there were baskets and baskets left over. The story of the loaves and fishes had been passed down orally for decades before it was chronicled by Mathew in the New Testament, Matthew Chapter 5, verses 3-12.[55] Joshua explained how it could have happened logically with no supernatural intervention—a sudden mass sharing event that was not planned but inspired by one man's words. It got me to wondering, *what if a food truck or catering company van suddenly pulled up right here in front of us and started handing out free food with no prior planning? Would that be considered a miracle? The*

---

55 The New American Bible, World Catholic Press, 1987, Matthew Chapter 5, verses 3-12, pp 1014-1015.

miracle of burritos and tortilla chips? What if that is how the miracle of the loaves and fishes happened but everyone after framed it supernaturally instead of as a sudden selfless flash mob of sharing? It all really depends on how you frame it.

The acoustics of the location permitted Joshua's voice to carry far up the hill, like in a Greek amphitheater or domed church. This is how Jesus conveyed his message to so many. Joshua used geography, science, and common sense to explain what many of us had only read in the Bible. His timing, theater, and words were impressive and moving. It was all in how he framed it, and he framed it convincingly well. He made Bible stories come to life and credible, even for those who were not religious. This was going to be a very memorable tour.

After the Church of the Beatitudes, we boarded the bus and then visited some ruins in Capernaum. Joshua had us sit on some broken pillars and foundational stones overlooking the Sea of Galilee. He explained that the Sea of Galilee probably looked like a small lake to Americans, but 2,000 years ago this was considered a large body of water—a sea—to the Israelites who lived around it. The spot where we were sitting was the ruins of St. Peter's ancestral home. Joshua set the mood again, speaking in simple Hebrew-accented English sentences. He had us all imagine that we were sitting in this exact spot about 2,000 years ago. Then a skinny, long-haired bearded guy in his late 20s, about the same age as most of the sailors on this tour, walked up and introduced himself. He was plain-speaking and not wealthy, but he asked you if you wanted to leave your home, your job, and your family to become a fisher of men. Many of you would have probably told him to f…off, but Peter and a few others were so captivated that they followed. Again, Joshua's story-telling and perfectly timed "F" bombs had their effect. Sailors were amazed and thinking, wondering, *is that how it really happened? Would I have told Jesus Christ to f…off or would I have followed him?*

We all felt like we had gone back in time. For a few seconds we all put ourselves in St. Peter's sandals and wondered what we would have done. At that moment in time Jesus was not the Jesus we understood now: he would have been just another guy from Nazareth whom nobody knew. Why did Peter and his friends follow him? What would convince us today to leave everything and go down what had to be a high-risk path, following a young unemployed, unknown preacher in Roman-controlled Judea. I could not imagine anyone convincing me to leave my family, my job, and my home in Jacksonville. Almost everyone listening to Joshua felt the same way. The fact that St. Peter and the other disciples decided to follow the unknown, unproven Jesus was the real miracle here.

After Capernaum, we travelled to Jerusalem, making a few stops on the way for snacks and lunch. The tour was going well, and I could see that our crew was enjoying the F bombs for Jesus tour. I was moved as well. I had grown up steeped in Roman Catholicism and believed in God and Jesus, but always had doubts and a hint of cynicism in the back of my mind. Critical thinking and religion did not seem to mesh well in my experience, but Joshua's "walking in the footsteps of Jesus"expedition was changing my thinking. His framing of the events and places made things feel real. Perhaps the Holy Land was truly holy after all.

236

Me on the F...bombs for Jesus tour Jerusalem, Israel March 2007

Some USS THE SULLIVANS (DDG-68) crew members
in Jerusalem, Israel March 2007

The tour continued and we entered Jerusalem after stopping for lunch. There we saw the Wailing Wall and walked the Via Dolorosa, the path that Jesus took to the crucifixion. We also visited the Church of the Holy Sepulchre, which was built on the site of Jesus's death and resurrection. History, religion, and the foundation of Western culture were right under our feet and all around us. George, Francis, Joseph, Madison, and Albert would have loved this tour. I imagine they would have liked our guide Joshua's plain-spoken, profanity-peppered stories. Joshua was able to communicate profound spiritual and philosophical ideas through simple sentences that rang true in our ears, hearts, and minds. The truth is the truth whether one is standing in front of the Wailing Wall or in Waterloo. The Sullivan brothers had been through a war with an enemy that was determined to fight to the death, just like Joshua. I could picture them all hamming it up and posing for a selfie with Joshua in front of the Dome of the Rock or at the entrance to the Garden of Gethsemane.

Joshua continued his tour with the same tone, explaining the history of the holiest sights on earth with humor and just the right amount of profanity so as not to be perceived as blasphemous by the religious amongst us. He was a subject matter expert and conveyed his message in precise plain language, which resonated with the crew. It was all in the way he framed it, and it stuck with us forever. Our crew had walked in the footsteps of Jesus and was transported back in time by Joshua's story-telling.

The F–bombs for Jesus tour was the best rendition of the New Testament I had ever heard. This one-day USO trip to Jerusalem would serve as a once-in-a-lifetime pilgrimage for many of us that day. It was emotional, educational, entertaining, and fun. And it was all in the way Joshua framed it.

CHAPTER 21

HONOR, FEAR, AND INTEREST

The Coloseum, Rome, Italy

USS THE SULLIVANS (DDG-68) arrival at Souda Bay, Crete 2007

Throughout my time aboard USS THE SULLIVANS (DDG-68), I had the good fortune to visit some of the most historic places in the history of Western civilization. Our crew had the priviledge and honor of representing George, Francis, Joseph, Madison, and Albert and the *We Stick Together* spirit in Carthage, Rome, Syracuse, and Jerusalem. We visited other historically significant locations such as Ireland, Denmark, Turkey, Romania, Georgia, Bulgaria, Croatia, France, and Spain. As we toured these ancient cites and historic places, we were awe-struck by their history, gravitas, and the very many lessons they could teach us.

In the Navy, after the mission is completed or the deployment ends, someone is tasked with compiling all the pertinent lessons learned. These lessons learned are written down, edited, and then turned into Power Point briefs and messages to be distributed to the fleet for posterity. Throughout this short work, that is what I have attempted to do.

I added in some sea stories as all sailors would for color and context. This is the tale of real people, USS THE SULLIVANS (DDG-68) sailors, not fictional characters in a play or movie. I am not a professional historian, learned scholar, or travel writer, but a simple sailor, the son of a fisherman, so please forgive me my trespasses if my grammar, phrasing, and tone lack elegance and sophistication. I am warning the reader now because what follows is my estimation of the lessons learned that fluttered through my mind as we walked in the footsteps of the ancient ones.

Ancient Greek ampitheater in Siracusa (Syracuse) Sicily near Augusta Bay

Thucydides was an ancient Greek historian and general who lived from 460 to 400 BC. He compiled the first, and arguably the best, lessons learned about human nature, warfare, and antiquity. USS THE SULLIVANS (DDG-68) utilized Augusta Bay, Sicily, and Souda Bay, Crete, as our home away from home during our deployment to the Mediterranean and Black Seas. These are the places Thucydides and the ancients lived, fought over, and documented in the first chapters of Western civilization. We stopped in both these ports many times—five times in Augusta Bay and four times in Souda—to be exact. We also visited Catania, Sicily; Naples, Italy; and Aksaz, Turkey, all locations where the ancient Greeks lived, fought, and died. Even for those in our crew who were not interested in history, the spirit and vibe of these places penetrated the soul and affected us all whether we realized it or not.

Thucydides was one of the first to accurately capture the events in these places, which made up what we recognize today as ancient Greece. Thucydides' best lessons come to us from his book about the Peloponnesian War between Sparta and Athens. Although Thucydides was an Athenian he made a point to try and write down his observations and analyses in an unbiased way. He was a critical thinker whose passion was the study of human nature and why people go to war. One of his greatest lessons was that men (and women too) fight because of honor, fear, and interests. His theory still holds for many today. People fight because of pride—honor; out of fear—they are afraid; and interest—they are greedy and want more stuff. Thucydides believed human nature did not change and that this was just the way mankind is. And while many have wished him to be wrong, brutal wars and destruction continue in our era because of honor, fear, and interests.

There were many other lessons that USS THE SULLIVANS (DDG-68) crew members noted as we sailed and stopped throughout what once was ancient Greece. Things that matter to modern and ancient sailors alike. Both Augusta Bay and Souda Bay had very deep natural harbors that were easy to navigate. The weather at both locations was sunny and pleasant, and there was an abundance of fresh fruits and vegetables. We also discovered that European tugboats do not push; they pull ships into position. It was much easier to get parts and technical support in Augusta Bay and Souda Bay because of the nearby U.S. Naval bases in Sigonella, Sicily, and at Souda Bay proper. Sailors tend to want to help their ship-mates, so stopping in these places afforded THE SULLIVANS crew better opportunities for repairs and administrative work like getting new sailors onboard and obtaining good medical support for those in need. Sicily and Crete happen to be the largest islands in the Mediterranean and centrally located. Both for the ancient Greeks and the U.S. Navy they proved to be fantastic hubs for supporting naval power.

The ruins of ancient Carthage in Tunis, Tunisia

From March 5-9 2007, USS THE SULLIVANS (DDG-68) was anchored a few miles off the coast of ancient Carthage near Tunis, Tunisia. The crew got plenty of opportunities to visit Tunis and Carthage as the winds kicked up and many of the crew were stranded ashore for three days.

Eventually the seas and winds calmed down and the crew was able to board ferries and return to the ship. In Tunis *We Stick Together* meant sailors had to share hotel rooms, food, and money until they could get back safely.

Carthage was a major player in the ancient world and fought a series of wars over Sicily from 460 BC to 315 BC, battling the Greeks. Carthage emerged as the leading maritime power in the western Mediterranean from roughly 300 BC until its destruction in 146 BC by Rome during the Punic Wars. The Carthaginians were also known as the Phoenicians. They were great sailors who explored the coasts of Spain, Portugal, and Britain. Phoenician ships and seamen circumnavigated Africa centuries before Magellan and other Portuguese explorers even dreamed of trying. The great success of Carthage ultimately led to conflict with another ancient superpower, Rome. Carthage fought Rome long and hard but ultimately lost and was destroyed. The ruins USS THE SULLIVANS (DDG-68) crew members toured are all that remains of the once great Carthage.

Elephant fountain in Catania, Sicily

So what are the lessons learned from Carthage? Location, location, location. In ancient geopolitics, modern warfare, and the real estate business, its all about location. Carthage was located on the exposed coast of North Africa and was constantly fighting for control over Sicily and the critical maritime trade routes in the Mediterranean. While anchored off Carthage (Tunis), USS THE SULLIVANS (DDG-68) was hampered by bad weather and high winds. Tunis harbor was too shallow for our ship, causing us to anchor out about 5 nm from fleet landing. We had a very difficult time getting our crew and supplies aboard near Carthage. Perhaps this same weather and geography hampered the Carthaginians. Any good U.S. Navy supply officer knows you need better logistical support than your enemies to win the war. Sicily provided both better logistics and safer natural harbors. We could understand why the Carthaginians wanted to take it over.

Carthage fought both the Greeks and the Romans, eventually losing out to Rome. Probably not a good idea to continually pick fights with super-powers. Eventually the odds will not be in your favor. Many of the crew were familiar with Hannibal, the Carthaginian general who battled Rome and crossed the Alps with elephants. In Catania where we stopped from April 6 to 9, 2007, there is a fountain of an elephant in the city's main piazza. Catania is known as the elephant city, and although this specific elephant is not technically connected with Hannibal's invasion of Italy, it did trigger thoughts of Carthaginian soldiers riding through the Alps on the backs of their war elephants to attack Italy from the north. Hannibal was a brilliant tactician and general. He defeated the Romans three times in Italy before being defeated trying to defend his hometown of Carthage. Fortune seemed to favor the bold when it came to the Punic Wars and the demise of Carthage. Luck and timing are also important variables for sailors.

The ancient Greeks and Romans believed in lots of different gods and deities. Caerus, also known as Kairos, was the Greek God of oppor-tunity—luck and timing. He was depicted as a handsome young man, always running, who had winged feet like Hermes or his Roman cousin, Mercury, the diplomatic, mediating God of commerce. For the ancient Greeks and Romans, luck and timing were essential facts of life, which they believed could be tipped in one's favor by worshipping and paying homage to the right supernatural beings. The ancient Greeks also wor-shipped the goddess Tyche (pronounced TIE–SSH), the God of chance. The Romans also had a similar female deity they called Fortuna, and believed *Fortuna caeca est* (Fortune is blind). *Wheel of Fortune* (Rota Fortunae in Latin) was not just a game show from the late 1970s—still hosted by Pat Sajak and Vanna White, but something Goddess Fortuna actually spun blindfolded, determining the fate of the fortunate and the unfortunate.

The crew of USS THE SULLIVANS (DDG-68) was highly aware of good luck and timing, especially with regard to a previous deployment, where the ship stopped in Aden for fuel in January 2000. USS THE SULLIVANS (DDG-68) was attacked by Al-Qaeda terrorists but did not know it. They believed the boat that was heading towards them and eventually sank was a contracted trash pick-up so the story goes. There for the grace of God go I; was it divine intervention, the luck of the Irish, or just luck and timing that saved USS THE SULLIVANS (DDG-68) that day? Unfortunately for USS COLE (DDG-67), Fortuna's Wheel of Fortune landed on death and destruction on October 12, 2000. The same Al-Qaeda terrorist cell that had attempted to blow a hole in the side of USS THE SULLIVANS (DDG-68) just ten months earlier had studied their lessons learned and succeeded with their deadly suicide boat attack at the same spot in Aden's harbor, killing 17 sailors, American heroes, like George, Francis, Joseph, Madison, and Albert Sullivan. Luck, timing, and location are crucial variables to the success or failure of all missions.

CHAPTER 22

MAINTAIN YOUR SENSE OF HUMOR ...THAT IS AN ORDER

Miami Dolphins Cheerleaders onboard USS THE SULLIVANS (DDG-68) September 2006

Serving in the U.S. Navy at sea in a destroyer is a lot of work and serious business. It can also be fun and exciting. As previously mentioned, it is all in the way you frame it. There were approximately 300 sailors in the crew of USS THE SULLIVANS (DDG-68) in 2006. When we were at sea and training, sailors would work 12 to 15 hours a day standing watch and doing their primary job and collateral duties as well. Staying focused and alert for so long causes stress and fatigue. All work and no play makes sailors accident-prone and unsafe. In USS THE SULLIVANS (DDG-68) maintaining your sense of humor was authorized and encouraged. A little laughter at the right time greatly reduces stress and alleviates anxiety. Research has proven that laughter reduces levels of stress hormones such as cortisol, epinephrine, and dopamine while elevating beneficial physiological effects like blood flow to the heart, healthy antibody production, and mood. If you want to be happier and live longer then laugh a little; that is an order.

Although most sailors will not admit it, fear and anxiety are present and real for those who work in maritime professions. Life at sea in a warship is difficult and dangerous. Fear permeates from working in an unstable environment, where you must keep your head on a swivel and always remain vigilant. Death and destruction could come in an instant. A Chinese- or Russian-made cruise missile launched from 10 nm away could be on top of you in 1 minute and 30 seconds. Or death might come while you are sound asleep in the middle of the night from a torpedo attack, as was the fate of our namesakes. The fear is real, and it is always present. The hero of Trafalgar, Vice Admiral Horatio Nelson, Royal Navy (1758-1805), recognized this, claiming, "I could not tread these perilous paths in safety, if I did not keep a saving sense of humor."[56]

USS THE SULLIVANS (DDG-68) was named in honor of five brothers who gave their lives for our nation. Their story was framed in a positive manner and used to sell war bonds and motivate the home front. The reality of how they died was a much darker tale involving explosions,

---

56 https://www.brainyquote.com/quotes/horatio_nelson_167961. Downloaded July 1, 2021.

dehydration, exposure, shark attacks, and drowning following a devastating torpedo attack on their ship by Japanese submarine I-26. Only ten sailors out of a crew of nearly 700 survived and all five Sullivan brothers were lost. There is nothing humorous in this tale. It was sad, heart-breaking, and tragic. But thatis not how George, Francis, Joseph, Madison, and Albert would want to be remembered. They were scrappy pranksters who enjoyed laughing and living life. They worked hard but had fun and maintained their sense of humor, as best we know, until they were lost. That is the way I like to remember them, and many in the crew felt the same way. They were just like us 64 years earlier. They were sailors in their 20s and I am sure they enjoyed a bawdy joke, a good laugh, and having fun ashore just like we did. They were no different, no better and no worse, than our crew. They stuck together until the end, and that is what we would do too while maintaining our sense of humor.

Humor is a divine gift. It keeps you sane when things get dark. Sharing a laugh bonds people together and breaks down barriers. It makes a slow watch pass by and prevents you from drifting off to sleep; it is hard to fall asleep when you are laughing. There is clearly a time and place for laughter—timing is everything. But laughter and humor are necessary for good order and discipline. Life at sea without laughter would be misery and just plain suck.

In USS THE SULLIVANS (DDG-68) each grouping of sailors in the formalized cliques or hierarchy of a ship had its own comedians and funny traditions. The wardroom, chiefs' mess, and mess decks all had their clowns and jokesters. In the wardroom in USS THE SULLIVANS (DDG-68), the "George" was the junior ensign. The officer with the newest lineal number and shortest time aboard was treated special. He or she had special ensign bars to wear on their uniform. Sometimes they even got a special parking spot on the pier. The George, along with the Bull ensign, the senior ensign on board who was formerly the George, had special duties and responsibilities generally associated with recreation and fun for the wardroom. The George and Bull were Navy traditions and helped break the tension and monotony of sea duty. They got tooled and fooled with quite a bit, but they brought smiles and happiness to many who needed it.

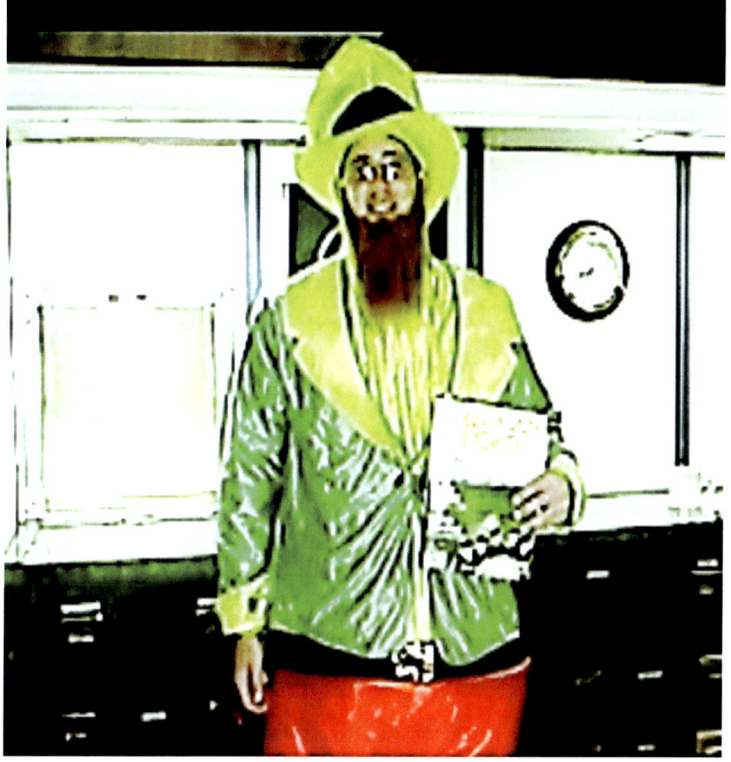

USS THE SULLIVANS (DDG-68) leprechaun costume

In USS THE SULLIVANS (DDG-68), we used the George ensign as the ship's mascot and would make him or her wear a leprechaun costume with a big hat and oversized shoes. The leprechaun would then have to dance an Irish jig on the forecastle (aka foc'sle, front of the ship near the bow) during underway replenishments or whenever called upon. The leprechaun was used like the Philly Phanatic, the San Diego Chicken, or Mr. Met to make the crew laugh and lighten things up a bit. This tradition of the Bull and George ensigns serves an important purpose and continues today on most U.S. Navy ships. It is just one example of U.S. Navy customs and traditions that accommodate the need for levity and humor.

People need humor and happiness. The ancient Greeks believed that happiness was the highest human good. They called this eudaimonia. Eudaimonia is a word you do not hear every day, but it means a positive flourishing, the individual happiness brought about by achieving one's true nature. It could also mean being blessed, ethical, and virtuous. In Aristotle's *Nicomachean Ethics,* written around 340 BC, the concept of eudaimonia was linked to the golden mean. The golden mean is about moderation and balance. People should strive to live their lives somewhere between excess and deficiency; think Goldilocks here: not too hot or too cold, but just right. Aristotle and his students used critical thinking to figure out how best to achieve happiness. He believed a virtuous person would be naturally disposed to behave in the right way for the right reasons, and, thus, derive happiness from behaving rightly. Today in the U.S. Navy this equates to the concept of integrity. When sailors do the right thing because it is the right thing to do, they will find happiness. Throw in a fun port call and a visit by the Miami Dolphins cheerleaders and happiness will abound.

Miami Dolphins Cheerleaders on bridge of USS THE SULLIVANS (DDG-68) 2006

In late September 2006, USS THE SULLIVANS (DDG-68) pulled into Port Everglades, Florida, for Fleet Week. USS THE SULLIVANS (DDG-68) was one of many U.S. Navy east coast ships that arrived for this annual event to honor the fleet and showcase the U.S. Navy to the taxpayers of South Florida. The Navy League organized events and entertainment for the sailors. As luck would have it, USS THE SULLIVANS (DDG-68) was selected to host the Miami Dolphins cheerleaders and participate in the pre-game festivities for the Miami Dolphins, who were hosting the Buffalo Bills that weekend for their opening home game.

The Dolphins cheerleaders were genuine and kind, and all had a good sense of humor. They brought smiles to the crew and posed for pictures and signed autographs. They would sneak into spaces and surprise our sailors who were working throughout the ship. They enjoyed their role as pranksters, and bringing happiness to the sailors on duty who could not leave the ship that particular day. The Miami Dolphins Cheerleaders were more than just pretty faces: they were truly professional and posi- tive. They took great pride in their work and purpose, demonstrating the concept of eudaimonia with their contagious positive spirit. They did their job well, and it showed.

Like our crew, they came from all over the United States and foreign nations as well. One cheerleader was from Japan and had her own Japanese press crew accompanying her onboard. Another was from Venezuela, and there were even a few from the local Miami area. They were genuinely happy and their photo ops and surprise appearances throughout the ship caused much laughter and many selfies, which would bring many future smiles and stories for our sailors for years to come.

The Navy League and the Miami Dolphins organization were kind and supportive of THE SULLIVANS crew. They rolled out the red carpet and provided us with VIP treatment. One of the highlights of our visit to Port Everglades was a behind-the-scenes visit to the Dolphins training facil- ities. Many in our crew got a private tour led by the Dolphins' coaching staff of their locker room, practice field, and private offices. Our junior sailors were surprised to see many of the same techniques and proce- dures we used aboard ship being practiced by professional athletes. Plans of the day, pre-planned responses, intense physical conditioning, and team meetings were just a few of the methods that NFL teams and the surface navy had in common.

The lesson learned here is that humor, fun, and laughter are necessary ingredients for effective warships, NFL teams, and any organization that wants to be successful. A little humor and fun can go a long way, especially when things are stressful and busy for those so far from home. Serving in the U.S. Navy is a lot of work and requires many sacrifices, but it can also be fun, especially when one is honored and treated with kindness, and cheerleaders.

CHAPTER 23

GOING HOME

USS THE SULLIVANS (DDG-68) departing on deployment Nov 27, 2006

St. Peter's Fiesta parade Gloucester, MA June 2007

Going home is something every sailor looks forward to. As our ship sailed closer and closer to Florida, discussions about what sailors would do the day they got home echoed through the passageways. I imagine it has always been this way. Stories about the journey home abound in history and mythology. The ancient Greeks believed Odysseus battled the cyclops and faced many obstacles placed in his path by Poseidon on his journey home. The legendary Roman military leader Lucius Quinctius Cincinnatus wanted to get home to his farm but first had to save the Roman Republic. His virtuous gesture of relinquishing power after he had won and returning home inspired others such as George Washington and Russel Crowe's fictional character Maximus Decimus Meridus in the 2000 Academy Award-winning film *Gladiator*. Going home is good. Going home can be virtuous and bring happiness-eudaimonia if you are an ancient Greek. In late May 2007, here is what I wrote in my captain's journal about going home:

captain's journal entry dated May 26, 2007

We are 3 days away from home... .crew a bit agitated and anxious. We all just want to go home. Six months away from family and friends is a long time. I need some time to reevaluate where we as a Navy family are headed. What is important to us and where we think we want to end up.

These were my thoughts as USS THE SULLIVANS (DDG-68) headed home from deployment. Six months can seem like an eternity when you are without your family. Our crew had sacrificed their time, talent, and effort to fulfill our mission, but our families had sacrificed too. They had to do it alone and get on with life while we were away. Reconnecting with loved ones after so long an absence takes time and patience. Responsibilities and roles shift and priorities change. Some relationships do not survive, and there will be sailors who need help and guidance from those of us who have faced heartbreak before. Time will be their friend and heal their wounds, but the first few weeks can be rough.

In my head I was concerned about not only our crew but my family as well. Going home meant that my tour as commanding officer of USS THE SULLIVANS (DDG-68) was coming to an end. This meant yet another move for our family. Navy life is nomadic and moving constantly is stressful and difficult, especially for teenagers and young children. In 2007, my wife and I had two kids under the age of 12 who had lived in Florida, Italy, California, and Rhode Island. They also had extended stays with our families in Illinois and Massachusetts in between our many moves. After this tour in THE SULLIVANS we would pick up and move again. This pattern was similar for many in our crew. It was a difficult lifestyle and part of the cost of a career in the U.S. Navy. Home for us was wherever we ended up together.

Coming home is a happy time. When USS THE SULLIVANS (DDG-68) pulled into Mayport after more than six months, there were plenty of hugs and smiles. Our rock band Keelhauled played their first U.S. gig, staging their equipment midships and playing as we entered port that day. There were tears of joy from spouses, families, and new parents. At least one THE SULLIVANS sailor that I saw dropped to one knee and proposed to his soul mate asking for her hand in marriage as soon as he walked off the brow. There were sailors who held their children for the first time and some that reunited with parents and friends. Returning home is a happy and joyous occasion, like Christmas day and a wedding reception meshed with a graduation party and a family reunion. It was nice to be home.

USS THE SULLIVANS (DDG-68) returned from deployment on May 29, 2007. The ship then had a two-week leave and stand-down period, where most of the crew took some much-deserved time off. The ship was underway again on June 12, 2007, and headed to New York City, NY; Norfolk, VA; and then to my hometown of Gloucester, MA. Getting underway at least once a month is good for maintaining qualifications and skills but can be taxing on family life. USS THE SULLIVANS (DDG-68) crew members were encouraged and permitted to take leave during these upcoming U.S. port visits, especially if they had family and friends nearby.

In New York City our ship sailed past the Statue of Liberty and laid a wreath at sea in front of the 9/11 memorial site. It was a moving patriotic act that brought tears to many eyes. USS THE SULLIVANS (DDG-68) has a special connection with New York City, specifically Staten Island, as there is a pier there named in honor of our ship. USS THE SULLIVANS (DDG-68) was commissioned into service in Staten Island on April 19, 1997. Staten Island was the ship's birthplace, making this visit a family reunion of sorts. New York City's annual Fleet Week celebration had happened just a few weeks earlier, leaving USS THE SULLIVANS (DDG-68) time alone to celebrate our successful deployment and return home in the Big Apple.

USS THE SULLIVANS (DDG-68) arriving in NYC in June 2007

Bagpipers play for USS THE SULLIVANS (DDG-68) arrival at Staten Island June 2007

In New York City, USS THE SULLIVANS (DDG-68) had a busy schedule. We were met by the ship's sponsor, Miss Kelly Sullivan, the grand-daughter of Albert Sullivan. We also hosted the first commanding officer of USS THE SULLIVANS (DDG-68) and held a retirement ceremony for him and his family. This too was a moving event highlighting over 10 years of USS THE SULLIVANS (DDG-68) history and adventures. Many members of the USS THE SULLIVANS Foundation also met the ship for tours and to reunite with old shipmates from both DD-537 and DDG-68. New York City felt like a home away from home, even for Boston Red Sox fans.

Following our trip to New York City, USS THE SULLIVANS (DDG-68) was on the move again, this time to Norfolk, where we helped train more than two dozen midshipmen for their annual summer training. Training never stops on any warship, and our now seasoned crew provided excellent underway replenishment, small arms, and damage control training to the midshipmen, hoping to sway them to become surface warfare officers. Training midshipmen brought back many memories for me. It felt like I had just done my summer midshipmen training (aka CORTRAMID), but that was more than 20 years ago. Carl Sandburg, an American poet and Pulitzer Prize winner, said "Time is the most valuable coin in your life. You and you alone will determine how that coin will be spent. Be careful that you do not let other people spend it for you."[57] I had given a lot of my coin to the U.S. Navy with no regrets, but now my family needed some as well. Our next port visit would provide that opportunity.

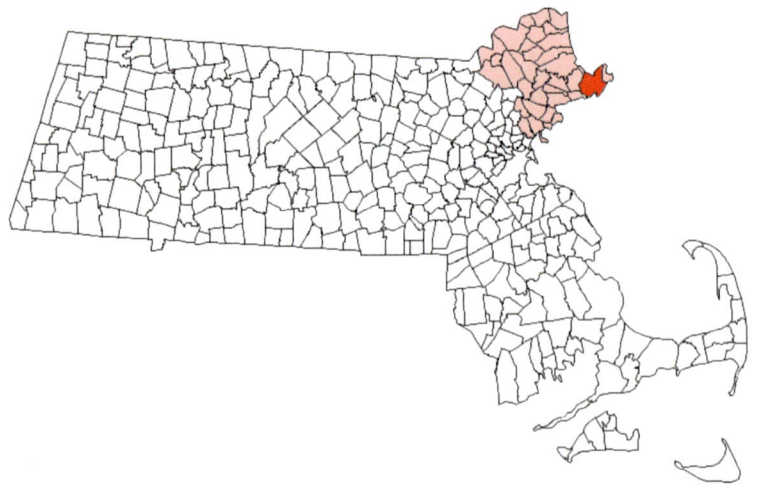

Gloucester, MA is the red area in the map of Massachusetts above

Gloucester is an old fishing town located on Cape Ann, 36 miles north of Boston. Gloucester harbor was first discovered by the French explorer, Samuel de Champlain in 1606. He called it Le beau port, as its natural harbor is beautiful. Gloucester was later settled in 1623 by some of

57 https://www.goodreads.com/author/quotes/16380.Carl_Sandburg#:~:text. Downloaded July 2, 2021.

the original pilgrims of the Plymouth colony. Some of these first English inhabitants likely hailed from Gloucester, England, and named the site after their home. Fishing had been its mainstay for over 375 years. I grew up here and all my family and friends from my youth lived here. I was going home and bringing all 300 of my THE SULLIVANS family with me. This would be the most memorable port visit of my life.

USS THE SULLIVANS (DDG-68) anchored in Gloucester with Boston in the background June 2007

On the morning of June 28, 2007, USS THE SULLIVANS (DDG-68) approached its anchorage just east of the Dog Bar Breakwater, which protected Gloucester Harbor. Our officer of the deck answered a hail from the harbormaster, whose voice sounded familiar. It was my father. My dad, James Parisi, served as an assistant harbormaster in Gloucester after he retired from fishing. His exchange with our female officer of the deck was entertaining and brought smiles and laughter to all who heard it. He wanted to talk to the captain, his son, and welcome him and the crew of THE SULLIVANS (DDG-68) home.

USS THE SULLIVANS' (DDG-68) mission in Gloucester was to support Second Fleet public relations tasking. Second Fleet's area of responsibility covered nearly 6,700,000 square miles and ranged from the North Pole to the Caribbean Sea. Visiting U.S. ports on the East Coast showcased the fleet to the public, made certain Congressional representatives happy, and supported U.S. Navy recruiting efforts in the Northeast. It also coincided with the annual St. Peter's Fiesta celebration.

Official St. Peter statue procession

Greasy pole competitor diving for flag

The St. Peter's Fiesta is a Gloucester tradition dating back more than 80 years, when many Sicilian immigrants came to Gloucester to work in the fishing industry, such as my great grandfather and grandfather. It is a five-day block party to celebrate St. Peter, the patron saint of fisherman, and the first Pope of the Roman Catholic church. Its roots and traditions are from Sicily, and it takes place in a neighborhood called the Fort near Gloucester's inner harbor and city center. This neighborhood was home to generations of Sicilian immigrants, including my father's family. The festivities include nine days of prayer, the blessing of the fleet, a religious-themed parade carrying the statue of St. Peter through the streets, and formal maritime-themed competitions like seine boat races and the famous walking of the greasy pole.

June 2007 greasy pole with USS THE SULLIVANS
(DDG-68) at anchor in background

The greasy pole is a fiesta favorite. Thousands of people come to watch this two-day competition that involves walking or running down a greased telephone pole suspended on a platform 20 feet over water 200 yards off Pavilion Beach in the inner harbor. The tradition came to Gloucester from Sicily, where competitive walking or climbing of a greased pole was an old custom and served as a test of courage and manhood for the courting of young Sicilian ladies. Competitors are encouraged to dress up as their favorite heroes, cartoon characters, or alter egos—for fun of course—and then must navigate their way 40 feet down a greased pole and capture the flag at the end. The competition results in thrills, spills, laughter, and sighs of dread, as many participants have broken limbs or concussed themselves before tumbling into the harbor. The winner gets a case of Budweiser and bragging rights.

In 2007, USS THE SULLIVANS (DDG-68) crew members were permitted to walk the pole despite not being of Sicilian origin or from Gloucester. This had never happened before in the history of the St. Peter's Fiesta that I was aware. But it was allowed because THE SULLIVANS crew members were considered part of my family. *We Stick Together* did not translate to some of our crew members' ability to stick to the greasy pole. They walked, slipped, and fell, but enjoyed their time and went into the history books as the only USS THE SULLIVANS sailors to ever walk Gloucester's greasy pole.

The crew of USS THE SULLIVANS (DDG-68) practicing
our rowing skills in a seine boat

USS THE SULLIVANS (DDG-68) crew members marched in the St. Peter's parade. Some of us also participated in seine boat races against the local U.S. Coast Guard station. We finished second but it was a close race that strengthened our *We Stick Together* spirit and ingratiated us with the local Coast Guard commander. USS THE SULLIVANS (DDG-68) color guard went to Fenway Park to present the colors and see the Boston Red Sox take on the Texas Rangers. Our rock band Keelhauled played some shows for the fiesta crowds in local bars and was a huge hit. The crew of USS THE SULLIVANS (DDG-68) were welcomed by the citizens of Gloucester as family because they were; they were my family, and I could not have been prouder of their conduct, character, and support.

CDR Tony Parisi, USN with family aboard USS THE SULLIVANS (DDG-68) in Gloucester

To this day the photos, memories, and mementos of USS THE SULLIVANS (DDG-68) participation in the 2007 St. Peter's Fiesta bring both a smile and tears to my eyes. All the feelings of happiness, success, pride, satisfaction, and joy come flooding back into my mind and heart. The tears well up when I think of the people that I loved and who help guide me on my life's journey that have since passed on and joined George, Francis,

Joseph, Madison, and Albert Sullivan in the next realm. The tears turn to smiles when I picture them altogether in the hereafter sharing a laugh and pointing down with pride at their ship, its crew, and all the people who were influenced by their words, deeds, and love. I believe *We Stick Together* holds true for this life and what comes after.

I also think of my family—both my immediate family and my THE SULLIVANS family. We came home together and all our hard work and effort was showcased for friends and family to see in Gloucester. The citizens of Gloucester were proud of one of their own, but also of all the crew of USS THE SULLIVANS (DDG-68). From my perspective, it was more joyous and jubilant than any Boston Red Sox World Series victory or New England Patriot Superbowl trophy parade. Our minor mission to support Second Fleet objectives would be the major highlight of my at-sea career. It was the emotional, spiritual, and natural apex to my time in command of USS THE SULLIVANS (DDG-68) and my career in the U.S. Navy. All the lessons learned from previous commands and tours had led me to this point. Fortune (or perhaps the Goddess Fortuna) had favored our crew and this ship. Our pursuit of excellence had taken us to the Black Sea and back, and now I was home. Tony Bennett might have left his heart in San Francisco as the old song goes, but I had left mine here in Gloucester and rediscovered it again in 2007.

I remember being very content with the trajectory of my life and our family's pursuit of happiness. In the future life would present many chal-lenges and tests, but for this one week in June 2007, everything had come together nicely and synchronized as if it had been scripted by George, Francis, Joseph, Madison, and Albert to showcase their ship in a profoundly personal manner to my friends and family here in Gloucester.

Gloucester is where I started my life's journey, and it was my home. My family and I would have to begin the next chapter of our Navy adventure soon, but for those few days in June 2007, we had achieved eudaimonia— we were truly blessed and happy. While digging through a scrapbook of these happy days, I came across a local newspaper with an article that quoted me saying, "We are a family in THE SULLIVANS and our ship's motto, *We Stick Together*, really helps get us through the tough times. I have seen incredible things in this ship—from Rome to Jerusalem to New York City. It has truly been an adventure." [58] Nothing tops going home.

---

58 "Native son proud to bring in USS THE SULLIVANS to Gloucester," Gloucester Daily Times, by Christina Morais June 28, 2007.

CHAPTER 24

Conclusions

*DDG-68 passing through the George P. Coleman
Memorial Bridge enroute to Yorktown, VA 2006*

When I sat down for the first time to begin the process of putting pen to paper to document the lessons learned from my time in command of USS THE SULLIVANS (DDG-68), I kept asking myself the same question over and over again in my mind: *18 years of service for 18 months in command; was it worth it?* If you were to ask a fiduciary or financial advisor this question, they would answer no. Had I put an equal amount of focus and effort into any other endeavor or profession I would have much more liquidity and a nicer 401K than I do now. This is true. But I did not seek a commission and volunteer to serve for 29 years in the U.S. Navy for the financial reward. I chose to serve because I believed in the Constitution, the United States of America, and the United States Navy. Becoming a surface warfare officer became my noble purpose, and the journey to command of USS THE SULLIVANS (DDG-68) forged my character and changed the arc of my life.

Sitting at my desk in my home and staring at the plaques, shadow boxes, and framed ship pictures that hung on the walls around me, I realized that what brought me the most happiness in life was sharing my most valuable lessons learned with others. Lessons learned can help us all on our journey through life. They nourish our curious souls and and help us find our way home. Sharing my lessons learned with the next generation of sailors would become my mission and purpose in life.

In USS THE SULLIVANS (DDG-68), every evolution, task, or mission required use of the PBED (plan, brief, execute, debrief) process. PBED is the cycle of how everything is done in all ships, submarines, aircraft squadrons, SEAL teams, and units throughout the U.S. Navy. During the debrief, the final stage, after the conclusion of the event, lessons learned are discussed. Lessons learned are the coin and corporate knowledge that the U.S. Navy depends upon to teach the next generation of sailors and continually improve the fleet. Navy lessons learned come at a high price and are often written in blood. They must not be forgotten and are very often overlooked. Disasters, accidents, and mistakes can be prevented if only people would take the time to read the lessons learned.

Modern warships like the USS THE SULLIVANS (DDG-68) cost over a billion dollars and are crewed by America's most precious resource: her selfless and patriotic young people. Sailors are human, and like all of us, will make mistakes. The U.S. Navy uses a specific philosophy known as Sound Shipboard Operating Principles and Procedures (SSOPP) to mitigate human error and pursue excellence, but sometimes that is not enough to prevent disaster. When mistakes happen, individuals and institutions need to be held accountable. The United States Navy cannot afford to repeat recent mistakes such as the deadly collisions of USS JOHN S MCCAIN (DDG-56) and USS FITZGERALD (DDG-62) in 2017, which resulted in the combined loss of 17 American sailors and hundreds of millions of dollars in repairs for both ships. There are many lessons learned in these two mishaps that we need to read and follow.

We Stick Together means we listen and learn from one another. We see things through to the end, do our homework, and strive for continual improvement along the way. We do not do things for fame and glory but to accomplish our mission and arrive home safely. As individuals we are responsible and accountable for our actions. We all need to work hard to develop our critical-thinking skills but also selflessly work together in synchronicity. Mission must always come first, before personal interests and career ambitions. The Golden Rule is always in effect and applies to all people all the time. Leaders should set the example and use their power to level the playing field so that good guys do not always finish last. We should all be simple kind of men and women, who try to love and understand the lessons learned in our own lives and from history. It is all there for us to find.

Looking back through the chapters of this work, I came to realize that the universe sends us all signals along our life's journey. Taking the time to observe and critically think through what is happening is a worthy investment of our time. Whether you walk in the footsteps of the ancients or listen closely to the lyrics of your favorite song, there are valuable lessons learned waiting to be uncovered. The truth is out there and its easier to find when *We Stick Together.*

The recurring theme throughout this short book revolves around the words, *We Stick Together.* This simple phrase taken from five American brothers who loved and supported one another to the bitter end has deep meaning for those of us fortunate enough to sail in the U.S. warships named for them. It is a simple truth uttered by average men who through their words, actions, and circumstance became transformed into American heroes. George, Francis, Joseph, Madison, and Albert Sullivan's spirit lives on in DD-537, DDG-68, and all the young men and women who have walked their decks. The Sullivan brothers represent all of us average Americans just trying to get home and do right by our family, our country, and our God. *We Stick Together* is about supporting one another in the darkest times. It also reminds us to be selfless and forgive those who have trespassed against us but not forget the transgressions. We must also maintain a sense of humor at sea and ashore. Laughter is a divine gift that helps us cope and ease pain and suffering.

Life is short and should be focused on the pursuit of happiness, or what the ancient Greeks called eudaimonia, the fulfillment of one's true purpose. Serving one's country and sacrificing for the benefit of others is a hero's journey that few are willing to make. For those who do, character and integrity become their most cherished and guarded resources. One's own character, guided by wisdom, passion, selflessness, and the pursuit of truth, is the basis of good leadership. As some of us trek down the path of life, we recognize that the most important lessons learned are just echoes of what we were taught in our youth. When our individual search for purpose in life is harnessed to the pursuit of excellence, success and eudaimonia naturally follow. True happiness is not about riches, fame, and glory, but finding one's noble purpose and the flourishing that comes from its pursuit.

Living in accordance with the Golden Rule and golden mean bring happiness, and does not require one to be an NFL athlete or ancient Greek hero. You may even encounter professional cheerleaders along the way that will brighten your day as you work hard to get better at the things you care about. Humor is a divine gift that reduces stress and helps us all through the toughest times. Remember the mnemonic device of the fancy French pickle (FFPIQL): formality, forceful backup, procedural compliance, integrity, questioning attitude, and level of knowledge. These tried and true principles and procedures will give you the confidence to remain calm and carry on while preventing and reducing human error.

Our ship's journey carried us to ancient and historic places where the lessons learned echo through time and helped guide us home. Even in the toughest times, when there was no sunshine or rainbows, the crew of USS THE SULLIVANS (DDG-68) remained optimistic and on the lookout for what the universe was trying to tell us. And in the end, when it was all said and done, a crew of individuals was able to stick together and complete all our missions. We had won, and in so doing we found that our journey had taken us home. Winning is sweet, but much sweeter when *We Stick Together*.

These are just some of the lessons learned I took away from my 18 months in command of USS THE SULLIVANS (DDG-68). I wanted to document our story and these lessons learned for posterity. I also wanted to provide a snapshot of what life was really like in USS THE SULLIVANS (DDG-68) and for U.S. Navy sailors in the surface warfare community.

Admittedly my perspective was framed by where I came from, how I grew up, and my own pursuit of excellence based on the values instilled in me by my family, my church, my college, and my Navy.

We Stick Together is a motto that resonated with me because it reflects the spirit of America I learned in my youth: E Pluribus Unum; United We Stand, Divided We Fall; and Live Free or Die. There are many such lessons learned throughout the U.S. Navy. I hope others will put pen to paper and share them with us. Thank you for your time and readership. Fair winds and following seas. Sail safe and keep smiling as you search for your noble purpose. Your journey may take you around the world where you will discover many lessons learned before it brings you home.

USS THE SULLIVANS (DDG-68) passing through
Istanbul, Turkey enroute to the Black Sea 2007

BIBLIOGRAPHY

Books

Aristotle, *Nicomachean Ethics,* Athens, Greece, 340 BC.

Aurelius, Marcus, *Meditations,* Rome, 170 AD.

Campbell, Joseph, *The Hero with a Thousand Faces*, New York City, New York, Pantheon Books, 1949.

Carnegie, Dale, *How to Win Friends & Influence People,* New York City, New York, Gallery Books, 1936.

Gladwell, Malcom, *Outliers*: *The Story of Success,* New York City, New York, Little, Brown and Company, 2008.

Orwell, George, *1984 A Novel,* London, England, Secker & Warburg, 1949.

Orwell, George, *Animal Farm,* London, England, Secker & Warburg, 1945.

Mack, William P. and Stavridis, James, *Command at Sea 5ᵗʰ Edition*, Annapolis, Maryland, Naval Institute Press, 1999.

Rand, Ayn, *Atlas Shrugged,* New York City, New York, Random House, 1957.

Rand, Ayn, *The Fountainhead,* Indianapolis, Indiana, Bobbs-Merrill Company, 1943.

Satterfield, John R., *We Band of Brothers, The Sullivans and World War II*, Parkersburg, Iowa, Mid-Prairie Books, 1995.

Swift, Jonathan, *Gulliver's Travels,* London, England, Benjamin Motte, 1726.

The New American Bible, Canada, World Catholic Press, 1991.

Thucydides, *History of the Peloponessian War*, London, England, Penguin Classics, 1972.

Tzu, Sun, *The Art of War,* China, 500 BC.

Washington, George, *Quotations of George Washington*, Carlisle, Massachusetts, Applewood Books, 2003.

West, Diana, *The Death of the Grown-Up: How America's Arrested Development is Bringing Down Western Civilization,* New York City, New York, St. Martin's Press, 2008.

Films

Bacon, Lloyd. *The Fighting Sullivans.* 20th Century Fox, 1944.

Cameron, James. *Titanic.* Paramount Pictures, 1997.

Donaldson, Roger. *No Way Out.* Orion Pictures, 1987.

Jordan, Neil. *Michael Collins.* Warner Brothers, 1996.

Landis, John. *The Blues Brothers.* Universal Pictures, 1980.

Lucas, George. *Star Wars Episode IV: A New Hope.* Twentieth Century Fox, 1977.

McKay, Adam. *Talladega Nights: The Ballad of Ricky Bobby.* Sony Pictures, 2006.

Milius, John. *Flight of the Intruder.* Paramount Pictures, 1991.

Scott, Tony. *Top Gun.* Paramount Pictures, 1986.

Spielberg, Steven. *Jaws.* Universal Pictures, 1975.

Spielberg, Steven. *Saving Private Ryan.* DreamWorks Pictures, 1998.

Articles

Feeney, Matthew, "Seventy Years Later, It's Still "1984," CATO Institute, June 5, 2019.

Graham, David A, "Rumsfeld's Knowns and Unknowns: The Intellectual History of a Quip," *The Atlantic*, March 27, 2014.

Morais, Christina, "Native Son Proud to Bring in USS THE SULLIVANS to Gloucester," Gloucester Daily Times, June 28, 2007.

Websites Visited

www.asq.orgwww.theatlantic.com
www.brainyquote.com
www.criticalthinking.org
www.dictionary.com

www.etymonline.com
www.goodreads.com
www.google.com
www.indymedia.ie
www.inspiringquotes.us
www.mentalfloss.com
www.merriam-webster.com
www.navy.mil
www.phrases.org.uk
www.shape.nato.int
www.pbs.org
www.en.wikipedia.org/wiki/Wikipedia
www.ynetnews.com

Miscellaneous Materials

Parisi, James, "Two Captains," Poem
Parisi, Anthony, USS THE SULLIVANS (DDG-68) private Capt's Journal July 05, 2005 to December 4, 2007.
U.S. Navy Sound Shipboard Operating Principles and Procedures circa 2004.

Unclassified Navy message, COMDESRON SIX ZERO dated 152057Z
MAY 07.

Unclassified Navy message, COMDESRON TWO FOUR dated 042013Z
DEC 07.

USS THE SULLIVANS (DDG-68) Plan of the Day, Saturday, April
28, 2007.

USS THE SULLIVANS (DDG-68) deployment video cruisebook
2006-2007.